The Most Inspirational Soccer Stories of All Time for Kids

15 Incredible Tales From Soccer History for Young Readers

Ryan Barkley

Table of Contents

CHAPTER 1: From Slum to Stadium: The Rise of Pelé, Brazil's Soccer Phenomenon 1

CHAPTER 2: A Decade of Dominance: Messi's Era in Barcelona...8

CHAPTER 3: The Hand of God and the Goal of the Century: Maradona's Duel with England.....................15

CHAPTER 4: The Gold Standard: Mia Hamm and the Rise of Women's Soccer 21

CHAPTER 5: The Underdogs' Triumph: Leicester City's Impossible Dream Season 27

CHAPTER 6: Captain America: Christian Pulisic's International Glory..33

CHAPTER 7: The Golden Boy: Mbappé's Quest for Global Supremacy 40

CHAPTER 8: The Triumph of Spirit: Cameroon's Indomitable Lions in 1990 46

CHAPTER 9: The Unstoppable Marta: Queen of the Pitch...54

CHAPTER 10: The Italian Renaissance: Azzurri's Road to Redemption in 2006...61

CHAPTER 11: The Invincibles - Arsenal's Unbeaten Dream..68

CHAPTER 12: Samba in Cleats: The Artistry of Neymar on the Pitch..77

CHAPTER 13: A FIFA Fairytale: Japan and the 2011 Women's World Cup..85

CHAPTER 14: Madeira to Madrid: The Making of Christiano Ronaldo..91

CHAPTER 15: Goalkeeping Glory: Tim Howard's Record-Breaking World Cup Performance.....................98

CHAPTER 1:

From Slum to Stadium: The Rise of Pelé, Brazil's Soccer Phenomenon

In a small Brazilian town, bustling with life and echoing with the sounds of samba music, there lived a young boy named Edson, though his friends called him "Dico." His home, Três Corações, was a place where the streets were a playground for kids with dreams bigger than their reality. Dico was one of these dreamers, a boy with a homemade soccer ball and a heart full of hope.

Dico's father, once a soccer player before an injury took him off the pitch, worked hard to make ends meet for their family. They didn't have much; luxuries were few and far between. Yet, Dico's father shared something more valuable with him than any riches could provide — the love and knowledge of soccer.

In those days, before the world buzzed with the glow of screens, soccer was a pastime that brought people together, a common language spoken with the feet. For Dico, it was more than a pastime. It was a whisper of the future, a promise that life could be something grander than the humble walls of his home and the unpaved streets of his town.

As he played in the dust, his feet painting masterpieces on the makeshift field, his friends cheered at a particularly skillful kick, and the name "Pelé" slipped out in the excitement. It was just a nickname, without meaning, an accidental twist of the tongue that would one day echo in stadiums, whispered reverently by millions.

Pelé's journey from the slums to the stadiums was as quick as one of his sprints down the soccer field. At the age of 15, when most kids his age were grappling with school and chores, Pelé caught the eye of a soccer scout. The scout was mesmerized by the young boy's artistry with the ball. It was evident that Pelé belonged somewhere his talent could soar, somewhere his name could be chanted by crowds.

He joined Santos FC, and the contrast between his past and present was stark. No longer was he the boy with the patchy soccer ball; now he donned a pristine uniform, his feet encased in proper soccer shoes, playing not just for himself, but for the roar of the fans that filled the stadium.

On the field, Pelé was a revelation. His youth belied a talent that seemed to come from a seasoned soul. He moved with an elegance that made the difficult look effortless, and the ball seemed to be an extension of himself, obedient to his command. He was not just playing; he was performing, and the pitch was his stage.

His first season with Santos was like a well-scripted play — where the young hero rises to meet his destiny. Pelé didn't just play soccer; he transformed it, leading the league in goals, a feat that left fans gasping and opponents humbled. His name became a chant, his exploits the subject of countless stories that filled the newspapers and the airwaves. Pelé was ascending, not merely to stardom, but to legend.

The boy who once played in the shadows of poverty was now a beacon of light, a symbol of possibility. The path from the slum to the stadium wasn't easy; it was paved with challenges, with sacrifices, with moments that tested his resolve. But for Pelé, every obstacle was an opportunity, every setback a chance to leap forward.

Pelé's incredible journey continued to unfold like a thrilling soccer match. With every game he played, he dazzled audiences with his remarkable skills. His fame spread far beyond the borders of his hometown, beyond the sandy beaches of Brazil, and into the hearts of soccer fans around the world.

He didn't just use his feet; Pelé played with his mind, always thinking two steps ahead of his opponents. He saw the field not just as patches of grass, but as a canvas where he could express his creativity and joy. For Pelé, soccer was an art, and he was its most devoted artist. His signature move, the 'Pelé run,' where he would dummy the ball past a confused goalkeeper, became something aspiring soccer players around the world would practice relentlessly.

The boy who had practiced with a sock-stuffed ball now faced goalkeepers who were the best in the business. Yet, even they often found themselves at a loss when Pelé had the ball. He would weave through defenses, a smile on his face, a spark in his eyes, and a determination in his heart. When he scored, the crowd would erupt in celebration, as if each goal was a victory not just for the team, but for everyone who had ever dared to dream.

As the youngest player in the league, Pelé brought more than just talent to his team; he brought a fresh spirit that reminded people why they loved the game. His youthful energy was infectious, and he quickly became the favorite not only among fans but also among his teammates, who saw him as a little brother with the extraordinary ability to inspire.

Off the field, Pelé was still just a teenager, with all the curiosity and vivacity of youth. He loved music and would often be seen with a guitar, strumming tunes that carried the rhythms of his homeland. He laughed easily and made friends wherever he went, his humble beginnings keeping him grounded despite his soaring fame.

His rise to soccer stardom was not just about scoring goals; it was about overcoming the odds. Pelé's story showed that no matter where you come from, no matter how tough life can be, there's always hope for something better. He became a symbol not just of success in sports, but of the idea that talent, hard work, and a bit of luck can help you achieve your wildest dreams.

But life at the top isn't without its challenges. With the spotlight firmly on Pelé, expectations soared. Every match he played, the pressure mounted. Was he going to score again? Could he lead his team to victory? The eyes of the world were watching, and with each step he took, the young star carried the weight of his country's dreams.

Pelé's legacy was growing with every season. He wasn't just a soccer player anymore; he was an icon, a source of national pride. Children all over Brazil laced up their shoes, took to the fields, and imagined themselves as Pelé, scoring the winning goal in a crowded stadium, the cheers of the fans ringing in their ears.

Pelé's legacy in World Cup history is monumental. At just 17 years old, he burst onto the international stage, helping Brazil claim their first World Cup trophy in 1958 in Sweden, a feat that instilled a sense of boundless pride and joy across his nation. His performances were so spectacular that he earned the Best Young Player award for the tournament. But Pelé's World Cup journey didn't stop there. He went on to be an essential part of Brazil's

1962 and 1970 World Cup-winning teams, becoming the only player in history to win three FIFA World Cup trophies. In these tournaments, his brilliance on the field was a catalyst for Brazil's triumphs, showcasing his extraordinary ability to deliver when it mattered most. His total of 12 goals in World Cup play remains a testament to his enduring talent and a pinnacle of success that players worldwide still aspire to reach.

At the club level, Pelé's impact was just as profound. Spending the majority of his career with Santos FC, he led the team to numerous victories, including two Copa Libertadores titles — the most prestigious club competition in South American football. His extraordinary tally of over 1,000 goals for Santos stands as a towering achievement in the history of the sport. Pelé's influence extended beyond the pitch; his presence catapulted Santos FC into being one of the world's most recognized clubs, as they toured internationally, playing against the top teams from Europe and elsewhere. Even after transferring to the New York Cosmos in the twilight of his career, Pelé's star power helped to spark a soccer revolution in the United States, elevating the sport's popularity to new heights and leaving a legacy that would impact the game globally for generations to come.

Yet, even as the goals and accolades piled up, Pelé remained focused on his love for the game. He didn't play for the records or the fame; he played because, for him, soccer was the purest form of joy. It was a connection to his childhood, to the dusty fields of Três Corações, and to the father who had first taught him to kick a ball.

Pelé's tale is one of magic, not just the magic he displayed on the field, but the magic that lives within every child who believes they can achieve greatness. Pelé's story reminds us that every champion's story starts somewhere, often in the most unlikely of places. For Pelé, it began in a small town, with a makeshift soccer ball and a dream as vast as the sky above Brazil.

CHAPTER 2:

A Decade of Dominance: Messi's Era in Barcelona

In a city known for its extraordinary architecture and rich history, a young boy from Argentina began to build something just as remarkable on the soccer fields of Barcelona. Lionel Messi, often simply known as Messi, wasn't tall, he wasn't big, but with a soccer ball at his feet, he was a giant. His story at FC Barcelona is like a soccer fairytale, filled with dazzling performances, unbeatable records, and trophies that would fill rooms. It's a story of how one player's skill and determination can change the game and how his decade of dominance made him a legend.

Messi arrived at Barcelona's famed youth academy, La Masia, at the tender age of 13. The academy was like a soccer school, except instead of learning about math or science, kids learned how to become soccer stars. Messi was far from home, in a new country, with a new language to learn, but when he played soccer, none of that mattered. On the field, he spoke a language everyone understood — the language of incredible soccer. It didn't take long for everyone to notice that Messi was special. He was so good that the coaches at Barcelona could hardly believe their eyes. They saw him not just as a future player for their team but as someone who could become one of the greatest of all time.

As Messi grew up, so did his skills. He went from playing with kids his own age to playing with men — professionals who had been in the game for years. But even they couldn't keep up with him. He was too quick, too clever, and just too good. When Messi was only 17 years old, he played his first game for Barcelona's main team, and from there, the records started tumbling one after another.

In Barcelona's colors of deep red and blue, Messi became a blur on the field, zipping past defenders as if they were statues. His feet moved so fast, controlling the ball with a magician's touch. The crowds at Camp Nou, Barcelona's massive stadium, would rise to their feet every time Messi got the ball, expecting something magical to happen — and he rarely disappointed. Whether he was scoring goals or setting them up for his teammates, Messi was the heartbeat of Barcelona.

During Messi's time with Barcelona, the club's style of play, famously known as 'tiki-taka', became a blueprint for soccer excellence. It emphasized skill, precision, and teamwork, all qualities that Messi had in abundance. Barcelona's dominance was reflected in their astonishing collection of silverware. They clinched the La Liga title an incredible 10 times with Messi at the helm, and their trophy room was a forest of silver and gold, from the Copa del Rey to the UEFA Champions League.

Messi, in the iconic Barcelona strip, wasn't just winning; he was redefining what it meant to be successful. He claimed the Ballon d'Or, the most prestigious individual soccer award, a record 7 times, etching his name in the halls of soccer history. His goal-scoring records were the stuff of legends — scoring an unfathomable 672 goals in 778 appearances for Barcelona, making him the club's all-time leading scorer by a wide margin. In the 2011-12 season alone, he set a European record by scoring 73 goals in all competitions, a figure that seems as untouchable as the stars.

Barcelona's rivalry with Real Madrid, known as 'El Clásico', was a stage that seemed custom-built for Messi's magic. He became the fixture's all-time top scorer, with 26 goals that often decided the fate of the match and, sometimes, the league itself. His performance was particularly spellbinding in March 2014, when he scored a hat-trick against Real Madrid, sealing a 4-3 victory and leaving fans and commentators alike searching for new superlatives to describe his talent.

The UEFA Champions League nights at Camp Nou saw Messi at his world-beating best. He guided Barcelona to 4 Champions League titles during his tenure, with one of the most memorable moments coming in the 2009 final against Manchester United, where he leaped above the defense to head home a goal, sealing a 2-0 victory. This was a remarkable feat for a player who is not known for his aerial prowess, demonstrating his versatility and relentless drive for success.

Messi's influence extended beyond mere numbers; it was the way he accumulated those figures—through mesmerizing dribbles, unthinkable passes, and goals that defied physics. His dribbling was a blur of movement that somehow propelled the ball forward as if it were tied to his laces. Defenders knew what was coming but could do little to stop it. He could change a game in the blink of an eye, with a sudden burst of speed or a moment of connection with a teammate that seemed telepathic.

Young soccer enthusiasts didn't just see a soccer player when they looked at Messi; they saw what hard work and perseverance could achieve. Behind every effortless dribble, every pinpoint accurate pass, and every goal that had fans leaping from their seats was a foundation of relentless training and an unwavering commitment to his craft.

As Messi grew older, he didn't slow down. Instead, he evolved, transitioning from a pure forward to a playmaker who could control the game's tempo and create opportunities for others as easily as he scored himself. He assumed the captaincy in 2018, leading with quiet confidence and continuing to be the driving force behind Barcelona's pursuit of glory.

Messi's legacy at Barcelona wasn't just built on what he did with the ball; it was also about the hope and inspiration he provided to millions around the world. His time at Barcelona showed that sports are about more than victories and losses — they're about the moments that take your breath away, the dreams they inspire in kids everywhere, and the memories that linger long after the final whistle has blown.

Under Messi's influence, Barcelona's style became synonymous with success and beauty in soccer. The team's philosophy, that winning was important but how you won mattered just as much, resonated across the globe. Messi embodied this philosophy every time he stepped onto the pitch, whether it was for a high-stakes Champions League match or a regular league game. His presence meant that no match was ever ordinary; there was always the chance to witness something extraordinary.

Messi's connection with his teammates was pivotal to Barcelona's success. He formed a particularly devastating partnership with Xavi and Iniesta, two midfield maestros who seemed to read his mind on the field. Together, they orchestrated plays that often culminated in Messi slicing through defenses to score. This golden trio was central to Barcelona's dominance, leading them to numerous trophies including a historic sextuple in 2009, when the team won the La Liga, Copa del Rey, UEFA Champions League, Spanish Super Cup, UEFA Super Cup, and the FIFA Club World Cup — all in one year.

His impact on the field was matched by his impact off it. The Barcelona youth academy, where Messi's journey began, saw an influx of young talents inspired by his story. They came in hopes of following in his footsteps, dreaming of scoring goals on the Camp Nou pitch, wearing the same jersey that Messi had made famous around the world.

Messi's years at Barcelona also included challenges, times when the team struggled, when the trophies eluded them, and critics wondered if his era was coming to an end. But Messi, with his characteristic resilience, would respond on the field, his performances silencing the doubters and reminding everyone of his genius. He adapted his playstyle as he matured, becoming as much a creator of goals for others as he was a scorer.

Even as records and opponents fell before him, Messi remained remarkably humble. He wasn't one for flashy celebrations; a smile, a fist pump, a hug from a teammate — these were his muted but genuine reactions to the moments of triumph. For Messi, the joy of soccer was in the play itself, in the camaraderie with his teammates, and in the cheers of the fans, young and old, who adored him.

By the time Messi concluded his chapter at Barcelona, his list of achievements was breathtaking. He had won 10 La Liga titles, 7 Copa del Rey titles, and 4 UEFA Champions League titles with the club. Individually, he amassed 6 Ballon d'Or awards while at Barcelona, a testament to his status as the best player of his generation, and for many, of all time.

Messi's era at Barcelona was a remarkable epoch in soccer history, a saga of skill, determination, and sportsmanship that will inspire countless generations to come. His story at Barcelona wasn't just about the trophies and the accolades, but about the journey of a boy with a dream who played his way into the hearts of millions, redefining greatness and leaving a legacy that transcends soccer. For kids reading this story, Messi's tale is a reminder that with passion, perseverance, and a love for the game, incredible things are possible.

As his Barcelona chapter closed, Messi's influence remained imprinted not just on the club, but on the entire sport. The city of Barcelona had become richer for his presence, its soccer story forever entwined with the diminutive Argentine who arrived as a shy teenager and left as a global icon. For fans, Messi's time at Barcelona was a golden era, a period of brilliance and beauty that will be retold for years to come, inspiring young soccer players everywhere to chase their dreams, no matter how impossible they seem.

CHAPTER 3:

The Hand of God and the Goal of the Century: Maradona's Duel with England

The story of Diego Maradona is one of magic and myth, a tale spun from the threads of his outlandish talent and the controversies that danced around him like shadows. For many soccer fans, Maradona was more than a player—he was a symbol of hope and human fallibility, a hero whose feet could create moments that seemed to stop time itself.

Our tale takes us to the sunbathed lands of Mexico in 1986, where the World Cup—a festival of soccer celebrated every four years—was in full swing. The world's eyes were glued to the games, where nations competed with a mix of nerves and excitement. Among all the soccer stars shining on this global stage, one man, Diego Maradona, captain of the Argentina national team, was about to engrave his name in history.

As Argentina prepared to face England in the quarterfinals, there was a feeling of more than just a soccer match brewing. It was a clash of titans, of history, and of pride. The match, set for June 22, was circled in calendars, with anticipation running high in the streets of Buenos Aires to the pubs of London.

Maradona was the focal point of such expectations. To the kids watching, he was not just a player; he was a superhero in cleats, a figure who made the impossible seem routine with his mere presence on the pitch. His every touch, every dribble, and every gaze towards the goal was a lesson in the art of soccer.

The Estadio Azteca in Mexico City was a fortress of excitement as fans poured in, faces painted with the colors of their country, hearts racing with the fervor of the moment. The first half was a tactical battle, a chess match played with a ball, where each team sought an advantage but found none.

Maradona moved across the grass with intent, his eyes alight with a mixture of focus and fire. Every time he received the ball, a hush fell over the stadium, as if the crowd was holding its breath, waiting for something extraordinary. He was marked closely by the English players, who knew that giving him space was like inviting a fox into the henhouse.

The first half whistle blew, and the score was locked at zero. Players from both teams walked off the field with their heads full of strategies and hearts full of ambition. Little did they know that the second half would contain moments that would be etched into soccer history forever, talked about and debated by everyone from seasoned commentators to kids playing in the backyards, dreaming of their moment in the World Cup sun.

In the Argentine locker room, Maradona was quiet, contemplative, almost as if he was visualizing the script of what was to come. The English team, on the other side, strategized on keeping him quiet, unaware that sometimes, plans mean little when faced with genius.

As the second half commenced, the stadium roared back to life. The players seemed more determined, knowing that a place in the semi-finals beckoned to those who dared to reach for it. Maradona, with his compact frame and low center of gravity, began to see more of the ball, his movements becoming more daring, more audacious.

The second half began with the intensity of a finale, a crescendo of chants, and cheers filling the air. Fans leaned closer to their television screens, their eyes wide with anticipation, witnessing a game that would become a fireside tale for generations.

Maradona was everywhere, a blur in blue and white, a spirit of the game incarnate. With each touch, he drew gasps from the crowd, his feet moving with a hypnotic grace, a precursor to the extraordinary.

Minutes ticked by, a silent tension building. It was a standoff. The English defense, a crew of determined guards, shadowed Maradona, yet he danced around them with a poise that spoke of a belief in something inevitable.

Then came the moment, the spark that would ignite controversy and brilliance in equal measure. A misjudged clearance from the English defense, a leap from Maradona, a meeting of flesh and leather - and the ball was in the back of the net. The stadium erupted, but the cheers were laced with confusion. Had Maradona outjumped the towering Peter Shilton to head the ball in? Replays would later reveal the truth, but in the moment, Maradona's quick glance towards the referee was the only hint of the mischief afoot.

The goal was allowed. The 'Hand of God', as Maradona would later cheekily name it, had cast its shadow. The ball had hit his fist before it hit his head, but the referees to did not see this illegal move at the time. The English players protested, but the scoreboard changed, and history was written in the most unusual ink.

Before the arguments could even settle, Maradona was at it again. This time, he would leave no room for doubt, no asterisk next to the brilliance about to unfold. He received the ball in his own half and turned, facing the length of the field. What followed was a performance, a masterpiece painted on the canvas of the Azteca.

With the ball seemingly tied to his left foot, he wove through the English defense. One, two, three - the defenders were left grasping at shadows, each step he took was a note in an epic symphony. The 60-yard dash felt like a lifetime, a slow-motion dance against the backdrop of frenzied spectators.

When he slid the ball past Shilton for the second time, the world knew it had witnessed the 'Goal of the Century'. The pure expression of joy on Maradona's face as he celebrated was a picture of the child within, playing the game he loved, in its purest form. The Argentine fans were delirious, the English stunned into a respectful silence, and children who dreamed of playing soccer knew they had just seen a goal they would replay in their backyards endlessly.

The match carried on, but those five minutes of magic and mayhem stood still in time. Maradona had lifted his team, not just on the scoreboard, but into the realms of legends, his name now whispered with a reverence reserved for the chosen few.

As the game proceeded, the unforgettable moments lingered in the air, making every pass, every tackle, and every shot charged with the electricity of what had already happened. Argentina held on, the defense as unyielding as the resolve that Maradona's magic had inspired. When the final whistle blew, Argentina had triumphed, and though there were other players on the pitch, it felt as though it was Maradona against the world, and Maradona had won.

In the days and years that followed, the 'Hand of God' goal would be debated fiercely. Was it a moment of cunning or a blatant flout of the rules? The 'Goal of the Century' would be replayed millions of times, each frame analyzed and admired, a testament to human skill and audacity.

But beyond the controversy and the acclaim, what lingered in the hearts of those who witnessed the match, especially the young fans, was the spirit of soccer that Maradona embodied that day. It was about more than winning; it was about the beauty and the flaws, the joy and the pain, the sheer unpredictability of life and sport.

Maradona's performance against England was more than a display of athletic prowess; it was a lesson in living and playing with passion and creativity, pushing the boundaries of what seems possible, and leaving a mark that time cannot erase.

For the children who drew inspiration from his feet, who would practice their dribbles and dream of their moment in the spotlight, Diego Maradona became a symbol of hope — a beacon that no matter where you come from, greatness awaits those who dare to chase it with a heart full of dreams and a relentless drive to achieve them.

CHAPTER 4:

THE GOLD STANDARD: MIA HAMM AND THE RISE OF WOMEN'S SOCCER

Before the stadiums roared with the energy of thousands and the names of female soccer stars became known in every household, there was a journey undertaken by a group of women who set out to redefine the beautiful game. At the heart of this revolution was a player whose name would become synonymous with women's soccer: Mia Hamm.

Imagine a field where the grass sways not just under the caress of the wind but also under the swift movement of a soccer ball. Here, a young Mia Hamm, with her ponytail swishing as decisively as her kicks, was not just playing a game; she was setting the cornerstone for a legacy.

Mia Hamm's story starts in a small town, where the fields are wide and the dreams even wider. From a young age, Mia had a ball at her feet, her companions the sun, the wind, and a boundless ambition. Children of her time often gathered around to watch her play, for even then, she had a spark – a way of moving, a way of commanding the ball that seemed beyond her years.

Her talent was undeniable, her dedication unwavering, and soon she found herself at the University of North Carolina at Chapel Hill, a place that would become her forge, the crucible where her skill would be honed to greatness. The Tar Heels' soccer program was a dynasty in the making, and Mia was its undisputed queen.

The college years were a blur of victories and accolades. Mia ran through defenses with a mix of grace and grit that left spectators in awe and opponents in her wake. Her team won national championships, and Mia collected awards that filled shelves and sparked the imaginations of young girls everywhere.

But Mia's ambitions weren't confined to the college soccer fields. She had her eyes set on a bigger stage: the international arena. And soon enough, she was wearing the colors of the United States Women's National Soccer Team, ready to show the world what she was made of.

As Mia Hamm laced up her cleats for the US Women's National Team, her eyes were set on a goal much larger than the soccer net: she aimed to elevate women's soccer to unprecedented heights. Every match she played was a stepping stone towards this aspiration. Her skill with the ball was legendary; she could dance past defenders with a swiftness that left crowds marveling and opponents grasping at shadows.

By the time the 1999 Women's World Cup arrived, Mia Hamm had become a household name. She had scored more than 100 goals for her country, a feat that etched her name in the history books. The '99 World Cup wasn't just a tournament; it was a defining moment for women's sports. The games unfolded like chapters in an epic saga, each pass and play building the narrative of a team destined for greatness.

The final against China was the climax of this saga. It wasn't just a match; it was a 90-minute rollercoaster of emotions, extending into extra time and culminating in the nail-biting suspense of a penalty shootout. Each player's approach to the penalty spot was a moment suspended in time, with Mia Hamm's kick being one of precision and pressure, demonstrating why she was already a two-time FIFA World Player of the Year by then.

The final penalty by Brandi Chastain, which secured the World Cup, became one of the most iconic moments in sports history. But the victory was more than just a shiny trophy; it was a crowning achievement following a tournament where the US team dominated, scoring a total of 18 goals and conceding only three, an emphatic statement of their superiority.

The legacy of that win and Mia Hamm's contributions to the game were far-reaching. It was about shattering perceptions and showcasing the raw talent and competitiveness of women's soccer. It gave rise to new leagues, brought in endorsements and sponsorships that were previously unheard of for women's sports, and inspired a generation to dream bigger. Mia Hamm retired with 158 international goals, an astounding record that stood as the highest tally for many years, and with 275 international appearances, she was a beacon of endurance and excellence.

The story of Mia Hamm and the '99 World Cup champions wasn't just about what they accomplished on the field; it was about how they changed the game off of it. Their victory echoed in the dreams of countless young girls who laced up their cleats and charged onto soccer fields, carrying the legacy of their heroes with every dribble and goal.

Mia Hamm's influence wasn't confined to the moments she spent sprinting across the pitch or scoring goals; it was deeply rooted in the culture she helped shape and the movements she inspired. After the whirlwind of the 1999 World Cup, women's soccer was no longer just a sport girls played – it became a passion that entire communities could rally behind, an arena where dreams could be pursued with fervor and a real sense of belonging.

Mia continued to play with relentless passion, always leading by example. She wasn't just a player; she was a mentor, a role model, and a symbol of what it meant to strive for excellence. Her impressive stats, like the 144 assists she provided over her career, spoke of her unselfish playstyle, always looking to uplift her team. It wasn't just about being the best; it was about making everyone around her better.

Even off the field, Mia's impact was huge. The Mia Hamm Foundation, which she founded after her brother's passing and her own experiences with bone marrow transplant, serves to raise funds and awareness for families in need of a transplant and continues to promote and develop young women in sports.

Her retirement in 2004 was an emotional moment, not just for Mia but for the sport as a whole. She left the game with two World Cup Championships, two Olympic gold medals, and countless other accolades, but perhaps her greatest legacy was the inspiration she provided to a generation of young players. The National Women's Soccer League (NWSL), established years later, stands as a testament to the growth of the sport she loved so dearly, and which she elevated through her incredible career.

In a stirring farewell match, children, some wearing jerseys with Hamm's number 9, watched as one of soccer's greatest chapters came to a close. Yet, in that ending was a new beginning, as those young fans walked away with dreams of their own, emboldened by the path Mia Hamm had blazed before them.

The story of Mia Hamm is more than a tale of personal triumph; it's a narrative that intertwines with the very fabric of women's soccer. It's a testament to how one individual's drive and determination can ignite change and reshape an entire sport's landscape. Her journey, marked by each dribble, each goal, and each victory, will forever be remembered as the gold standard in women's soccer – a standard that encourages young girls to not just dream, but to dream big, work hard, and believe in the impossible.

As the final whistle blew on Mia Hamm's playing career, the echo of her influence did not fade. It only grew louder, reverberating through stadiums, across fields, and into the hearts of aspiring athletes everywhere. And while the chapters of her career may have concluded, the story of her impact – much like the sport she transformed – continues to unfold with each new generation that takes to the field, inspired by the legend of Mia Hamm.

CHAPTER 5:

The Underdogs' Triumph: Leicester City's Impossible Dream Season

O nce upon a recent time, in a city nestled in the heart of England, there lived a soccer team not known for greatness or glitzy trophies. This team, known as Leicester City or the Foxes, was the kind of team whose greatest hopes often lay not in winning championships but in simply playing well enough to not be relegated to a lower league.

Our story begins in the summer of 2015, a time of new beginnings, when the warm winds of August whispered of possibilities. Leicester City had barely escaped relegation the previous season, finishing 14th out of 20 teams. The world of soccer expected them to struggle again, but within the quiet confines of their stadium, known as the King Power Stadium, something stirred.

The Foxes, under the guidance of their genial new manager, Claudio Ranieri, a man with kind eyes and a wry smile, who spoke of dreams with the quiet conviction of someone who believed in miracles, embarked on their journey. Ranieri didn't promise his team the stars; he simply asked them to work hard and to work together.

August turned to September, and the leaves began to change color, mirroring the unexpected transformation taking place in Leicester City's performances. Games that were expected to be losses turned into draws and victories. The players, many of whom were not household names, played with a fierce determination and a joy that was infectious.

Among these players was Jamie Vardy, a striker with a rags-to-riches tale fit for a storybook. Vardy, who had spent years toiling in the lower leagues of English football, found his stride. With every goal he scored, his confidence soared, and his name began to be chanted not just by Foxes fans but by soccer lovers who admired an underdog making good.

Then there was Riyad Mahrez, a wizard with a soccer ball, who could dance past defenders with a grace that left spectators in awe. Together with Vardy, they became a duo that struck fear into the hearts of their opponents.

But what is a team without its defense, the steadfast guardians of the goal? Leicester City's defense, led by the indomitable Wes Morgan, was like a fortress that grew stronger with every match. They weren't flashy, but they were effective, turning away assaults from the opposition with a calmness that belied the pressure of the situation.

As autumn leaves gave way to winter's chill, the Foxes' continued their steady climb up the ranks of the Premier League table. Fans whispered in hushed tones, hardly daring to believe what was unfolding before their eyes. With each game, the impossible seemed slightly less so.

In the crisp air of Saturday afternoons, when the stadium was a sea of blue, children hoisted atop their parents' shoulders would chant the names of their newfound heroes. The city of Leicester echoed with the cheers and songs of victory, resonating with a hope that had long been dormant.

In the heart of this team was a spirit that seemed unbreakable. The players fought for every ball, ran for every cause, and when one fell, another was there to lift him. This was not the soccer that was known to the world of glitz and glamour; this was soccer in its purest form, fuelled by passion and a camaraderie that money couldn't buy.

Their home, the King Power Stadium, became a fortress where dreams were forged into reality. Week after week, teams from across the land, laden with accolades and star players, came to face the Foxes on their turf, and one by one, they left with heads bowed, the magic of Leicester City too powerful to contain.

The cold of winter began to fade, and with the arrival of spring, a question hung in the air – could they really do it? The title was within reach, a prize so precious, yet for so long it had seemed unattainable for a club of Leicester's standing.

The media frenzy grew with every match. Cameras flashed, pundits analyzed, and former skeptics became believers. The team, once the subject of relegation fears, was now the headline of every story. But within the camp, the message remained consistent – take each game as it comes, play for each other, and let the football do the talking.

Every goal scored by Vardy, every dribble by Mahrez, every save by Schmeichel, and every tackle by Morgan wrote a new page in what was fast becoming the greatest story in modern soccer. The unity and the fighting spirit of the Foxes drew not only admiration but affection from fans all over the world.

As the end of the season drew near, the dream that had seemed so faint and so far away was now close enough to touch. The players, etching their names into soccer history, were not just winning games; they were winning hearts.

The city of Leicester was abuzz with anticipation as the final games approached. The blue jerseys of the Foxes were worn with pride in every corner of the city, and the streets hummed with the songs of hopeful fans. It was a collective breath-holding, a shared dream on the cusp of being realized.

As spring blossomed into full view, the story of Leicester City unfolded with each game, not just as a hopeful tale but as a testament to what unity and sheer determination could achieve. The team, which had started the season with odds of 5000-1 to win the Premier League, was edging closer to turning the fantasy into fact.

With two games remaining, the Foxes were perched at the top of the table, seven points clear of their closest rivals. Their nearest challengers, Tottenham Hotspur, faced a tough match against Chelsea, and as fans across the world watched with bated breath, the outcome of that game held the key to Leicester's triumph.

On May 2, 2016, as the final whistle blew at Stamford Bridge, confirming a draw between Tottenham and Chelsea, the impossible was achieved. Leicester City were declared Premier League champions. The Foxes had won the league with 81 points, 10 points clear of second-placed Arsenal, having won 23 games, drawn 12, and lost just 3. It was a fairytale ending to a season that had captivated the imagination of not just their fans, but soccer aficionados worldwide.

Jamie Vardy, the talismanic striker, had scored 24 goals, a figure that earned him the Premier League

Golden Boot. Riyad Mahrez's magical performances won him the PFA Players' Player of the Year award. Kasper Schmeichel, the goalkeeper, had kept 15 clean sheets throughout the season, a testament to Leicester's solid defense which conceded only 36 goals – the third-best record in the league.

As the team lifted the trophy, the city of Leicester erupted into jubilation. Children wore their Leicester jerseys with pride, mimicking Vardy's speedy runs or Mahrez's mesmerizing dribbles in playgrounds and backyards. The victory parade drew an estimated 240,000 people, more than a third of the city's population, all there to catch a glimpse of the players who had made the unimaginable happen.

The story of the 2015-2016 Leicester City squad is not just a collection of statistics and records; it is a narrative of hope, belief, and the undying spirit of the underdog. It is a chapter in soccer history that will be told and retold for generations, a reminder that sometimes, the heart and the will to fight can triumph over the size of the bank account or the roster of superstars.

And for every child dreaming of playing soccer, Leicester City's miraculous season stands as an inspiration that on the field of play, anything is possible – that with teamwork, dedication, and a bit of magic, dreams can indeed come true.

CHAPTER 6:

Captain America: Christian Pulisic's International Glory

Once upon a time in Hershey, Pennsylvania, a city known for its chocolate factory and sweet delights, a young boy named Christian Pulisic began to weave his own story, one that would take him far beyond the reaches of his small-town beginnings. This boy had a dream, a ball at his feet, and a heart filled with passion for the beautiful game of soccer.

Christian didn't just play soccer; he lived it. Every kick against the rugged walls of his home, every sprint in the cool, dewy mornings, every goal on the school soccer field wasn't just for fun; it was a step towards a future he was painting with each swish of the net. His parents, both athletes themselves, knew the gleam in his eye wasn't just the reflection of the stadium's floodlights—it was the spark of a burgeoning talent, waiting to burst into a blaze.

It was in these early years that Christian learned the value of discipline, the importance of practice, and the thrill of a well-placed pass. He watched the world's greatest players on television, imitating their moves, their strategies, and even their goal celebrations on the field. And as he grew, so did his dreams. They stretched from the local fields across the Atlantic to Europe, where soccer wasn't just a pastime; it was a way of life.

When he was barely a teenager, a pivotal decision loomed on the horizon. Scouts had seen something in him, something special. Christian was offered a chance to join the prestigious youth academy of Borussia Dortmund in Germany. It meant leaving behind his family, his friends, and everything familiar. But it also meant stepping closer to his dream.

Christian's arrival in Germany was like the opening pages of an epic tale. There, he was not just another American trying to play soccer; he was a young man with a vision, one who would wake up earlier, train harder, and run faster. He was on a mission to prove that his American spirit could thrive in a land where soccer legends were made.

His skills on the ball were mesmerizing, his pace was electrifying, and his soccer IQ was beyond his years. Christian didn't just adapt to the European style of play; he embraced it, enhanced it, and made it his own. With each game for Borussia Dortmund, he etched his name into the hearts of fans, and with every goal, he sent a message home: an American was here to stay, here to make waves in the soccer world.

Back in the U.S., young fans began to follow Christian's journey. They'd wake up at odd hours just to watch his games live, cheering every time he touched the ball, feeling a surge of pride every time he succeeded. Christian wasn't just playing for himself; he was playing for every kid who had ever been told that soccer wasn't America's sport, for every young player who had been overlooked, for every dream that seemed just out of reach.

As he continued to dazzle on the club stage, it was his time with the U.S. Men's National Team that would introduce him to a new moniker, one that would stick with him — Captain America. But his ascension to this title and his adventures wearing the red, white, and blue were just beginning.

The tale of Captain America, the moniker lovingly bestowed upon Christian Pulisic, truly began to unfurl as he gained experience with the U.S. Men's National Team. His debut was nothing short of a fairy tale; at just 17 years of age, he was the youngest American to play in a World Cup qualifier. With eyes wide and heart pounding, Christian stepped onto the pitch, not merely to play, but to etch his story into soccer history.

His start was remarkable, bursting onto the international scene with the raw energy of youth and a talent that seemed honed by years beyond his age. The stats began to tell a story of their own: with each cap,

Pulisic's influence on the game grew exponentially. He wasn't just a participant; he became the pulse of the team, the beat to which American soccer found its rhythm. By the age of 22, Pulisic had already netted 16 goals for his country and had become a talisman for creating opportunities for his teammates.

What made Pulisic special wasn't just his speed or his impeccable control over the ball—it was his audacity to take on players, to make the impossible seem mundane. His agility and his ability to read the game turned him into a creator, a player who could conjure goals from the slimmest of chances. Christian's style was poetry in motion; every touch, turn, and shot was a verse that spoke of his growth, of his journey from the fields of Pennsylvania to the stadiums where legends are revered.

Each goal he scored was a stitch in the fabric of his legacy, but it was not just about the figures. The true measure of his impact was in the moments of magic that left fans gasping, the bursts of brilliance that commentators could barely keep up with, and the look of sheer joy on the faces of children who now had an American hero to emulate.

Pulisic's story with the USMNT was about breaking records, yes, but also about breaking barriers. As the youngest ever to captain the USMNT in the modern era, he shouldered the hopes of a nation with the ease of a veteran, leading by example and rallying his team with a belief that resonated beyond the locker room.

And then came the matches that turned into legends — the nights when Captain America led the charge. Take, for instance, the CONCACAF Nations League final in 2021 against Mexico. The match was tied, the clock was ticking, and the air was thick with anticipation. In the 114th minute, a penalty kick was awarded to the USMNT. Pulisic stepped up, the weight of history upon him. With a steely gaze and a nation's breath held in unison, he struck the ball into the net, securing a 3-2 victory and a trophy for his team. It was a moment that transcended statistics; it was a chapter in a growing legend, a testament to his leadership, and a beacon of glory for soccer in the United States.

As Christian Pulisic's legend grew, so did his influence on the pitch. He wasn't just a player; he became a symbol of American grit and talent, a beacon for all those young athletes who dared to dream big. His move to Chelsea FC in the English Premier League — a league known for its intense competition and global following — was a step into a larger world, a test of his abilities and a chance to shine on one of the grandest stages in club football.

At Chelsea, the stats once again began to speak volumes of his caliber. His debut season in the Premier League saw him netting goals and providing assists, but it was the way he played that captured the hearts of fans. He didn't shy away from challenges; he welcomed them. In the 2019-2020 season, Pulisic ended with an impressive tally of 9 goals and 4 assists in the league, a remarkable feat for his first year in one of the most demanding leagues in the world.

But perhaps the most compelling chapter in Pulisic's story at Chelsea came in the form of the 2020-2021 Champions League. It's a tournament where legends are born, and Pulisic was set to make his mark. He showed a remarkable level of skill and composure, helping lead his team through the knockout stages and into the finals. He became the first American player to score in a Champions League semi-final, etching his name into the record books and showcasing his talent on one of the most prestigious platforms in club soccer.

His performances were more than just a personal triumph; they were a source of national pride. When Chelsea lifted the Champions League trophy after defeating Manchester City in the final, Pulisic had not just won a medal for himself; he had lifted the aspirations of an entire nation. He showed that an American could not only compete but excel at the highest levels of international club football.

The journey of Christian Pulisic, from his humble beginnings in Hershey to the grandeur of European stadiums, is a narrative of inspiration. It tells a story of a young boy who chased a ball with a dream and became a man who carried the hopes of a nation on his shoulders. It's a story that resonates with every strike into the back of the net, every sprint down the wing, and every wave to the cheering fans.

As Christian Pulisic continues to carve his path through the soccer world, the chapters of his legacy multiply. With every game, he writes new lines of possibility, of the potential within every young player who looks up to him. And while the stats may capture the breadth of his achievements, the true measure of his impact lies in the hearts of the fans and the dreams of children playing soccer across the United States, all of whom see in him the reflection of their own potential.

CHAPTER 7:

THE GOLDEN BOY: MBAPPÉ'S QUEST FOR GLOBAL SUPREMACY

In the bustling suburbs of Paris, there was a boy whose feet danced with the soccer ball as if they were born to do nothing else. This boy's name was Kylian Mbappé, and he was destined to become one of the most thrilling soccer players the world had ever seen. His story is not just about the goals he scored or the records he broke; it's about the joy he brought to the game and the dreams he inspired in the hearts of children all around the globe.

Kylian's journey began with a dream, a ball, and a boundless love for soccer. By the age of 6, he was already turning heads at the local club AS Bondy, coached by his father. His skills were extraordinary, his pace lightning-fast, and his passion undeniable. Even at such a young age, Kylian wasn't just playing; he was performing, and the soccer field was his stage.

As he grew, so did his reputation. By the time he was 12, he was invited to join the prestigious Clairefontaine academy, a place where France's most promising young talents are nurtured. Here, amidst the lush green fields and with the finest coaches, Kylian's potential began to take a definitive shape. His stats were impressive for a youngster: he was scoring goals at a rate that even seasoned professionals would envy, and his assists showed a player who was not only a finisher but a thoughtful team player.

The world first took serious notice of Kylian Mbappé in 2017. At just 18 years old, he helped lead AS Monaco to their first Ligue 1 title in 17 years. His contributions were phenomenal: 26 goals in all competitions, making him one of the youngest players ever to hit such a figure. But it wasn't just the number of goals; it was the style with which he scored them—each one a blend of speed, composure, and sheer brilliance.

However, this was just the prologue to what would become an epic saga. The soccer universe watched as Mbappé made the move to Paris Saint-Germain (PSG), one of the world's most storied clubs. There, under the bright lights of Paris, Mbappé's star shone even brighter. He was not just a young talent anymore; he was a leading actor on the world stage. His first season with PSG saw him net 21 goals and deliver 16 assists across all competitions, a stunning debut that earned him accolades and the adoration of fans.

The tales of Kylian's exploits on the soccer field read like the pages of a superhero comic book. One particular story that stands out is his World Cup debut in 2018. The world watched, some with bated breath, others with skeptical eyes, as this teenager stepped onto soccer's biggest stage. But pressure was like water off Mbappé's back — he played with a freedom and a joy that belied his years. With every darting run, every fearless dribble, and every composed finish, he was not just playing in the World Cup; he was redefining what it meant to be a 'wonderkid'.

His performances at the World Cup were nothing short of legendary. With four goals, including one in the final against Croatia, Kylian became the second teenager, after Pelé, to score in a World Cup Final. His name was etched into history, his legacy already taking shape as he lifted the trophy with his teammates, a beaming smile upon his face that told the world he knew this was just the beginning.

Kylian Mbappé's heroics at the World Cup were a herald of the golden times to come. As the seasons rolled on, his role at Paris Saint-Germain evolved. He was no longer just the phenomenal young talent; he became the team's lynchpin, the one who could turn the tides of a game with a single moment of brilliance. With every match, he was rewriting the rules, setting new standards, and pushing the boundaries of what was possible on the soccer field.

His stats were starting to tell a story of their own. In the 2018-2019 season, he scored an astounding 33 goals in

Ligue 1, becoming the league's top scorer. He wasn't just scoring ordinary goals; he was scoring goals that left fans gasping for breath — the kind that you'd rush home to try and replicate on your game console, the ones you'd talk about for days on end at school.

Mbappé's influence was extending beyond the field. His quick feet, keen eye for goal, and infectious smile were making him the face of soccer for a new generation. He was a constant fixture on magazine covers, his jerseys were worn by kids in the streets of Paris and beyond, and his social media was a window into the life of a new kind of soccer idol — one who was as much about style and substance off the pitch as on it.

But it wasn't just about the fame or the flashy lifestyle. Mbappé was, at his core, a competitor. He thrived on the roar of the crowd, the thrill of the game, and the joy of victory. He was a team player, one who celebrated every assist with as much gusto as his own goals. And as PSG chased the elusive Champions League trophy, Mbappé was front and center, leading the charge.

In the 2019-2020 season, the Champions League campaign was a rollercoaster. It was during this time that Mbappé's resilience shone through. Even when things didn't go as planned, when injuries threatened to sideline him, he came back stronger. In the knockout stages, his performances were crucial, leading his team to the final for the first time in the club's history. Although PSG didn't lift the trophy, Mbappé's reputation as a world-class player was solidified.

Off the pitch, Mbappé knew the power of his platform and used it to inspire change. He donated significant sums to charity, met with children from all walks of life, and spoke out on important issues. He wasn't just a soccer player; he was becoming a leader, an example of how talent coupled with character could make a difference in the world.

Mbappé's journey from a young boy with a ball at his feet to a global superstar is a testament to where talent, hard work, and passion can lead. With each chapter of his career, he has not only raised the bar for the next generation but has also etched his name among the legends of the game.

For every kid out there kicking a ball around in the backyard, dreaming of scoring the winning goal in a World Cup final, Kylian Mbappé's story stands as a shining beacon of possibility. It tells them that it's okay to dream big, to set your sights on the stars because, with dedication, those dreams are within reach.

In the pages of soccer history, the chapter on Kylian Mbappé is one that will be revisited over and over again, not just for the breathtaking goals and the dazzling runs but for the spirit he embodies. His story is one of relentless pursuit of excellence, a reminder that every time we step onto our fields of dreams, we carry with us the potential to make history.

As Kylian continues to write his legacy, young fans around the world don their jerseys with his name on the back, hoping to channel just a fraction of his brilliance. And perhaps, somewhere among them, is another young talent, ready to start their own story, a story that one day might be told alongside Mbappé's.

CHAPTER 8:

The Triumph of Spirit: Cameroon's Indomitable Lions in 1990

In the summer of 1990, a soccer team from the heart of Africa set out to do the unthinkable. The Cameroon national team, nicknamed the Indomitable Lions, was about to shake the foundations of the football world in the most spectacular fashion at the World Cup in Italy. Cameroon was not a country many had placed bets on; they were considered underdogs, a team that should be happy just to participate. But oh, how wrong the doubters were!

The story of Cameroon's Indomitable Lions is one of courage, unexpected twists, and the sheer joy of the game. It was in Italy that these Lions showed the world that in soccer, the size of the nation or the fame of its players does not dictate the passion and the power that can emerge when eleven players unite with a single heartbeat for their country.

Before the tournament even began, the Lions were training hard, knowing they faced a colossal challenge. They were pooled in a group that sent shivers down the spine of even the most seasoned teams, set to face the likes of Argentina, the defending champions with the legendary Diego Maradona as their captain. Yet, within the team's camp, a quiet confidence was building, a belief that they could achieve something extraordinary.

The streets of Cameroon buzzed with excitement as families gathered around radios and televisions, all hoping for a miracle. Little did they know that their team was about to deliver a performance that would turn them into national heroes and global sensations.

As the opening match approached, the world waited to see what this team from Cameroon had to offer. Would they succumb to the pressure, or would they rise to the occasion and stun the football giants? The answer to that was eagerly anticipated as fans from across the globe tuned in to witness the unfolding drama of a World Cup that was about to be rocked by the spirit and determination of the Indomitable Lions.

The opening match was a scene set for a story that would reverberate through time. Cameroon, a team ranked far from the top in the world standings, were pitted against Argentina, the reigning world champions, led by the man who was perhaps the world's most awe-inspiring footballer, Diego Maradona. On paper, it looked like a mismatch, a straightforward game for Argentina. Yet, the Indomitable Lions had other plans.

As the teams took to the field, the tension was palpable. The stadium was a cacophony of noise, with fans from both sides drumming up an atmosphere of anticipation. The whistle blew, and the match that was supposed to be a formality became a showcase of Cameroon's resilience and tactical discipline.

The game was a defensive masterclass from the Cameroonian side. They thwarted wave after wave of Argentinian attacks with a combination of physical strength and sharp tactical awareness. The stats began to tell a story of their own. Argentina, with their superstar Maradona, had the lion's share of possession, but the Cameroonian defense stood firm, repelling an impressive 12 shots on goal.

Then, the moment that defied belief came in the 67th minute. François Omam-Biyik rose higher than the Argentinian defenders and, with a powerful header, sent the ball towards the net. The Argentinian goalkeeper got a hand to it, but the ball had a will of its own, bouncing over the line and into the goal. It was a goal that would be replayed over and over.

The statistics showed that Cameroon only had a few shots on goal, but that was all they needed. They had capitalized on their chance, a testament to their efficiency and determination. But the drama was far from over. The game took a turn when two Cameroonian players received red cards, reducing them to nine men on the field. It was a test of endurance and spirit, and what a test it was.

With two fewer players, Cameroon's defense transformed into an impenetrable fortress, each player channeling the spirit of a nation that refused to be beaten. Argentina pushed forward, but the scoreline remained 1-0 in favor of Cameroon until the final whistle blew, cementing one of the most astonishing upsets in World Cup history.

The match stats painted a picture of a game dominated by Argentina in everything but the score. Yet, it was the heart and spirit of the Indomitable Lions that the world would remember. Cameroon had only three shots to Argentina's 23, but they scored where it counted. They ran fewer kilometers, made fewer passes, but each action was laden with purpose and fight.

That day, Cameroon didn't just win a soccer match; they won the hearts of millions and inspired a belief that on the football pitch, the impossible could become possible.

After the seismic victory against Argentina, Cameroon's reputation in the tournament changed overnight. They were no longer just participants; they were contenders. The victory had been a fusion of skill, strategy, and sheer will, and it ignited a belief within the team that they could go toe-to-toe with the world's best.

The next challenge was Romania, a skilled European side that could not be underestimated. Cameroon approached the match with the same tenacity that had served them well against Argentina. The game was tough, a real test of stamina and nerve. But Cameroon held on with a robust defensive performance complemented by quick counter-attacks. The match statistics would tell you it was evenly matched, each side with their share of possession and shots on goal.

This time, it was Roger Milla, the veteran striker, who stepped up to etch his name into World Cup lore. Coming off the bench with his trademark energy and charisma, Milla scored twice, showing that age was no barrier to excellence on the soccer field. His goals sealed a 2-1 victory for Cameroon, and with that win, they became the first African team to reach the quarter-finals of a World Cup, a monumental achievement that sent waves of pride across the continent.

Cameroon's last group match against the Soviet Union was a rollercoaster of emotions, with the Lions already through to the next round. The game ended in a 4-0 loss, but it did little to dampen the spirits of the team or their supporters. The statistics from that game would show more shots and more attacking play from the Soviet side, but the Lions had already done enough to progress, and their eyes were firmly on the knockout stage.

In the Round of 16, Cameroon faced Colombia, another game that would become a testament to their resilience. It was a tight affair, with both sides cautious not to give away any advantage. After a goalless 90 minutes, the match went into extra time. It was then that Milla, the hero from the previous game, once again danced his way through the opposition defense to score two decisive goals, securing a 2-1 victory for Cameroon.

The stats from that match showed Cameroon having fewer shots on goal than Colombia, but they were clinical in their finishing. Milla's goals were a display of efficiency, taking his chances with precision and calm under pressure.

Cameroon's quarter-final match against England was where their remarkable journey reached its peak. The Lions were not overawed by the occasion or their opponents, taking the lead through a penalty converted by Emmanuel Kundé and then again through a goal by Eugène Ekeke. England, however, managed to claw back with two penalties, the second one in extra time, to win 3-2. The match statistics showed an evenly matched game, but it was England's experience and perhaps a touch of fortune that saw them through.

Cameroon's World Cup adventure ended there, but they returned home as heroes. Their performance had defied the stats and the odds. They had not just competed; they had captivated, not only proving that they belonged on the world stage but also setting a precedent for African teams in future World Cups. Their spirit and joy for the game had captured the imagination of fans around the world, leaving a legacy that would inspire generations to come.

The echoes of Cameroon's exploits at the 1990 World Cup resonated far beyond the stadiums of Italy. They had played with an infectious joy, a spirited camaraderie that drew in fans from across the globe. Their performances on the field had been a vivid tapestry of skillful plays, unyielding determination, and the kind of heartfelt passion that encapsulates the beautiful game. As children in Cameroon played soccer in the streets, they no longer just imagined themselves scoring the winning goal in a local match; now they dreamed of emulating their heroes on the world's biggest stage, scoring goals in a World Cup.

Cameroon's 1990 World Cup journey was more than just a series of matches; it was a narrative that transcended soccer. It spoke to the underdog in everyone, to the possibility of achieving the impossible with belief and hard work. Their story was not just about the goals scored or the games won, but about the barriers broken and the stereotypes challenged. They had redefined what an African soccer team could achieve, and in doing so, they inspired a continent and charmed the world. The Indomitable Lions had become immortal in soccer history, their legacy a testament to the unifying power of this global sport.

CHAPTER 9:

The Unstoppable Marta: Queen of the Pitch

In the vast and vibrant world of soccer, there's a name that rings out like a strike from the halfway line, a name that's written in the stars of the sport's history: Marta. But before she became the queen of the pitch, Marta Vieira da Silva was just a girl from a small town in Brazil with big dreams and an even bigger talent.

Marta's journey began in Dois Riachos, a place that seemed worlds away from the glittering stadiums where soccer legends are made. It was here, in the streets and makeshift pitches, that she first cradled a soccer ball at her feet, showing a natural talent that outshone her peers. Her early play was a prophecy of the greatness that was to unfold; even then, her deft touch and dazzling footwork were a whisper of the future queen of soccer.

As a young girl, Marta faced many challenges. Soccer was seen as a boys' game, and she often played with and against boys, because there were no girls' teams. But she was unstoppable, her feet dancing with the ball as if they were one. Her skill was undeniable, and soon, she was outplaying the boys, her name becoming known for her talent, even at such a tender age.

Her move to the city of Rio de Janeiro in 2000 when she was just 14 was like a story plucked from a fairytale. Here, she found the opportunity to play for a women's team, and it wasn't long before her performances caught the eye of scouts from all over Brazil. Marta was not just playing; she was performing, each match a symphony of soccer brilliance that left spectators spellbound.

By the age of 16, Marta's name was beginning to echo beyond Brazil's borders. She was called up to the Brazilian Women's National Team, where her impact was immediate. In her debut international season, she scored goals with a frequency that belied her youth, showing a composure on the ball that many seasoned professionals would envy. Her stats began to build: in her first 10 games, she scored an impressive 12 goals, a strike rate that heralded the arrival of a new soccer prodigy.

Her ascension was meteoric, and it wasn't long before Marta was showcasing her talent on the global stage. At the 2003 FIFA Women's World Cup, a tournament that gathers the planet's finest teams, Marta announced herself to the world. Though Brazil did not win the tournament, Marta's performances were a silver lining, her graceful play a testament to her burgeoning reputation as a world-class talent.

Marta's soccer journey was like a dazzling dribble through defenders – full of twists, turns, and moments of sheer brilliance. As she grew in skill and fame, her goals weren't just changing the score of the game; they were changing the game itself.

In 2004, a year after her World Cup debut, Marta played in the Athens Olympic Games. There, with the world watching, she scored goals that seemed to come from another planet. Her incredible speed, agility, and precision helped lead Brazil to the final, where they took silver. It was a heart-pounding tournament for Marta, who at only 18, was already playing with the poise of a veteran.

As the years went on, Marta's list of accolades grew longer and more impressive. She was named FIFA World Player of the Year five consecutive times from 2006 to 2010, a record that showcased her consistent excellence. She wasn't just part of the conversation for the best female soccer player – she was the conversation.

Her stats read like a dream: Marta scored over a hundred goals for Brazil, a feat that stands tall in the world of soccer. For her clubs, she was just as lethal. Playing for Umeå IK in Sweden, she netted 111 goals in just 103 appearances, a striking rate that would leave any soccer fan wide-eyed with wonder.

But numbers only tell part of the story. Marta's influence stretched beyond the grassy pitches. She became a symbol of perseverance and determination. Wherever she played, from Sweden to the United States, she brought a flair and joy to the game that inspired girls and boys alike. She showed that with enough passion and hard work, anyone could aspire to greatness, regardless of their background.

Marta's skill with the ball was magical, but her leadership on and off the field was equally important. As captain of the Brazilian national team, she didn't just lead with words; she led by example. In high-pressure situations, with the weight of her nation's expectations on her shoulders, Marta played with a mix of fiery competitiveness and cool composure.

The impact Marta had on women's soccer is immeasurable. She played a pivotal role in bringing more attention to women's soccer, fighting for equality and respect. Through her achievements, she demonstrated that the women's game deserved the same recognition as the men's. Marta wasn't just playing for herself or even just for Brazil; she was playing for every girl who was told soccer wasn't for them.

Marta's story is more than a tale of personal triumph; it's a series of unforgettable moments that have marked the history of soccer. One such moment came during the

2007 FIFA Women's World Cup, where she exhibited a performance that would become part of soccer folklore.

In the semi-final against the United States, Marta showcased her extraordinary talent. With the ball at her feet, she danced past defenders with a finesse that seemed almost effortless. Her signature move, a quick change of direction that left her opponents scrambling, was on full display. In that match, she scored two goals, the second of which was a masterpiece of control and poise, helping to secure a 4-0 victory for Brazil.

Her performance in the 2007 World Cup was so stellar that she not only won the Golden Boot for being the tournament's top scorer with seven goals but also the Golden Ball for being the best player. These awards were a testament to her incredible skill and impact on the game at the highest level.

Beyond the awards and the accolades, what truly makes Marta's story resonate with fans, especially young ones, is her relentless pursuit of excellence against all odds. She has become a beacon for perseverance in sports, showing that with talent and determination, barriers can be broken.

Marta's influence on the pitch also transformed how the world viewed women in soccer. She didn't just score goals; she broke down prejudices, fought for recognition, and paved the way for future generations. Her advocacy off the field, especially for equal pay and better conditions for women in soccer, has been as powerful as her strikes on goal.

Yet, for all her success and activism, Marta remains humble. She often speaks about the joy of playing soccer and the love she has for the game—a love that is evident every time she steps onto the field. Her passion is infectious, inspiring young girls to lace up their cleats and chase their soccer dreams with the same fervor.

Despite her growing list of accolades and her burgeoning reputation as one of the greatest to ever play the game, Marta's journey was never free from obstacles. Her path was strewn with the same prejudices and dismissals that many women in sports face. But it was her response to these challenges that cemented her legacy as much as her on-field brilliance.

Marta was often compared to her male counterparts, a comparison that, while meant to compliment, also hinted at the underlying bias toward women's sports. Yet, she never allowed these comparisons to overshadow her identity as a player. She was not the "female Pelé"; she was Marta, a soccer player with her own unique style and achievements.

This unwavering sense of self was evident in her leadership on and off the field. As captain of the Brazilian national team, she didn't just lead by example with her exceptional play; she also became a vocal advocate for her teammates and for the broader community of female soccer players worldwide. Marta used her platform to call for greater investment in women's soccer, better infrastructure, more opportunities for young girls, and equality in how women's soccer was promoted and covered by the media.

Her advocacy work took on various forms, from public speeches at prestigious events to intimate soccer clinics for young girls in Brazil and beyond. She partnered with organizations dedicated to sports development and gender equality, always with the message that every girl deserves the chance to play, to compete, and to dream.

On the pitch, her legacy continued to grow. Marta became the first player, male or female, to score at five different FIFA World Cups when she netted a penalty against South Korea in 2015. And then, in the 2019 World Cup, she extended that record with her 17th goal, becoming the tournament's all-time leading scorer.

But stats and records only tell part of Marta's story. Her influence can be measured in the stadiums filled with young girls wearing her jersey, in the increasing viewership numbers for women's soccer, and in the shifting conversations about women in sports. Every goal Marta scored wasn't just a point for her team; it was a strike for equality.

CHAPTER 10:

THE ITALIAN RENAISSANCE: AZZURRI'S ROAD TO REDEMPTION IN 2006

The tale of Italy's road to redemption in the 2006 World Cup is one not just of soccer, but of heart, determination, and the unifying power of a nation's love for the beautiful game. It was a time when Italy, known as the Azzurri for their azure-blue jerseys, would rise from the ashes of scandal and disappointment to reach the pinnacle of the soccer world. But to understand the depth of this victory, we must first look back at the shadows that loomed over the Italian team as they entered the tournament.

Before the World Cup even began, the Italian soccer scene was rocked by a massive scandal. Allegations of match-fixing involving several of Italy's top clubs threatened to overshadow their World Cup campaign. It was a dark cloud that hung over the players' heads, many of whom played for the clubs embroiled in controversy. But within that storm, the Azzurri found a silver lining, a cause to unite them: they would play not for their tarnished clubs, but for the honor of their country.

As they embarked on their World Cup journey in Germany, the Italian team was not considered the favorites. The squad, led by veteran coach Marcello Lippi, was a mix of experienced warriors like captain Fabio Cannavaro and rising stars like Francesco Totti. Italy's opening match was against Ghana, a team with less history in the World Cup but abundant in talent and energy. It was a test, not just of skill, but of the Italians' ability to put scandal aside and play with the pride and tactical discipline their country was known for.

In a display of classic Italian defense paired with opportunistic attacking, Italy secured a 2-0 victory over Ghana. Goals from Andrea Pirlo, whose precision passing would become a hallmark of Italy's play, and Vincenzo Iaquinta showcased Italy's clinical finishing. But it wasn't just about the goals; it was the way Italy controlled the game, with Cannavaro, the rock-solid defender, making crucial interventions, and Gianluigi Buffon, the goalkeeper, demonstrating why he was considered one of the best in the world.

The win was a vital first step, but it was the next matches that would test the Azzurri's resolve. A hard-fought draw with the United States, where they played with ten men for nearly an hour, and a convincing win over the Czech Republic, saw Italy top their group. They were gaining momentum, but the real challenges lay ahead in the knockout stages.

With every game, Italy's play seemed to mirror their journey: disciplined, determined, and united against the odds. The Round of 16 saw them face Australia in a nail-biting match that was decided by a penalty in the final moments, converted by Totti. Then came Ukraine in the quarter-finals, where Italy's class shone through in a 3-0 victory, with goals that encapsulated their blend of defensive solidity and attacking flair.

As children following the tournament, each victory was a chapter in a story that seemed to be building to an unforgettable climax. Italian fans, from the cobblestone streets of Rome to the sunny shores of Sicily, began to believe that maybe, just maybe, their team could go all the way, could make them proud at a time when pride in Italian soccer was at a low point.

And so, Italy marched forward, toward the semi-finals, against the hosts, Germany. This match would test the Azzurri's mettle like no other. It was not just a clash of two soccer powerhouses, but a battle of wills, played out on the grassy stage of Dortmund's stadium. The tale of this titanic clash, and the dramatic journey towards the final, was unfolding to become one of the most memorable in World Cup history.

The semi-final match between Italy and Germany was not just a test of skill; it was a contest of patience and nerves. The German team, buoyed by the roars of their home crowd, played with a fervor that could inspire any sportsman's spirit. Italy, however, responded not with flamboyance, but with composure — a testament to the Italian style of 'Catenaccio', a tactical system emphasizing a strong defensive setup and counter-attacks.

As the match unfolded, it was clear that both teams were evenly matched. The Germans, with their precise play, and the Italians, with their impenetrable defense, kept the scoreboard unchanged as the minutes ticked away. The tension in the stadium was palpable, and for the young fans watching, it was a lesson in the emotional power of sport — every pass, every save, and every tackle was a stroke in the larger picture of this dramatic encounter.

The game edged into extra time, and with it came the real drama. Children and adults alike were on the edge of their seats, as Italy began to press harder, sensing that the German armor could be pierced. Then, in the 119th minute, just as the specter of a penalty shootout loomed large, Fabio Grosso curved the ball into the German net with a left-footed sweep that would etch his name into the annals of World Cup history. A mere two minutes later, Alessandro Del Piero, the veteran striker, sealed the deal with a second goal, sparking scenes of Italian jubilation and German heartbreak.

Italy's victory over Germany was more than just a soccer triumph; it was a victory of spirit, a showcase of mental fortitude that galvanized a nation back home, still reeling from the domestic soccer scandal. It was a victory that told every child with a dream of soccer glory that no obstacle was too great, no adversity too daunting, when hearts played in unison for a cause greater than themselves.

With the final whistle of the semi-final, the Italian team not only secured their spot in the World Cup final, but they also claimed a place in the hearts of millions, teaching a timeless lesson about the power of unity and the importance of never losing faith.

As Italy prepared for the final against France, anticipation reached fever pitch. It was to be a clash of titans, a final that promised to be a fitting conclusion to the Azzurri's roller-coaster journey in the 2006 World Cup.

The stage was set for a memorable showdown: the Olympiastadion in Berlin, draped in a mosaic of colors from the thousands of fluttering flags, awaited the final act of the 2006 World Cup. Italy, the resilient warriors throughout the tournament, faced off against a French team led by the legendary Zinedine Zidane, who was playing the final match of his illustrious career.

For any young fan learning about the beautiful game, this match was a treasure trove of lessons. The game wasn't just a test of talent; it was a chess match where strategy, patience, and moments of individual brilliance would determine the outcome. As the referee's whistle signaled the start of the match, the intensity could be felt through the television screens.

The early stages of the game brought an unexpected twist when a penalty was awarded to France. Zidane stepped up, exuding the confidence of a man who had been at this apex before. With an audacious 'Panenka' chip, he sent the ball into the net, and it was as if the ball itself hung in the air for a moment before descending, deciding the gravity of the moment. But Italy didn't have to wait long for their response, as Marco Materazzi headed in the equalizer from a corner. The score was level, and so were the emotions across both nations, waiting with bated breath.

As the game progressed, both teams had chances, but it was the defenses that stood firm. Italian goalkeeper Gianluigi Buffon and French defender Lilian Thuram became the personification of resilience, denying the opposition any clear route to glory. For young viewers, these moments underlined the importance of defense, often overshadowed by the allure of attacking play.

The game, locked at a stalemate after regular and extra time, moved on to the nail-biting finale of a penalty shootout. It was here that Italy showed their nerves of steel. With each successful penalty, the dream came one step closer to reality. And when French player David Trezeguet's shot hit the crossbar, the collective heart of Italy skipped a beat.

Finally, it was left to Fabio Grosso, the hero from the semi-final, to deliver the coup de grâce. As he struck the ball into the net, the Italians erupted in ecstasy. They had conquered the world of soccer, and they had done so by showcasing the full spectrum of their footballing philosophy — solid defense, strategic play, and seizing the moment when it mattered most.

The victory in the 2006 World Cup was not just a redemption for the Italian national team; it was a beacon of hope for a nation in turmoil, a narrative of triumph that would inspire countless youngsters in Italy and around the world. It taught them that sometimes, the journey is fraught with challenges, but with unity, resilience, and belief, the summit can be reached.

And as the Azzurri lifted the World Cup trophy under the Berlin sky, their story became etched into the hearts of the young and old, a tale of overcoming the odds, a reminder that in the realm of sports, fairytales are not just possible, they are perennial. The saga of the 2006 Italian team would go down in history, not merely as a list of matches won but as a chronicle of the human spirit prevailing against all expectations.

CHAPTER 11:

Tʜᴇ Iɴᴠɪɴᴄɪʙʟᴇs - Aʀsᴇɴᴀʟ's Uɴʙᴇᴀᴛᴇɴ Dʀᴇᴀᴍ

As autumn winds began to swirl around the historic city of London in 2003, a sense of anticipation filled the air. In the bustling borough of Islington, the storied soccer club Arsenal was preparing to embark on what would be an unforgettable journey through the English Premier League.

The story of Arsenal's season didn't start with a trophy or a title, but with a quiet belief within the walls of their training ground. Under the guidance of their manager, Arsène Wenger, a man known for his philosophical outlook on soccer and his innovative approach to the game, Arsenal was shaping up to be a team with a unique blend of experienced grit and youthful zest.

As the leaves turned golden, the Gunners, as Arsenal's team is affectionately known, set out with a single, seemingly modest goal: to win their next game. But each victory sowed the seeds of something greater, and a pattern began to emerge. Game by game, win by win,

Arsenal's players were knitting together a campaign that was starting to look... different.

One of the early signs that this season was going to be special came with the flashes of brilliance from Thierry Henry. Henry, a striker from France with a dancer's grace and a poet's vision for the game, had the ability to do things with the soccer ball that made crowds gasp. Whether he was weaving through defenses like they were statues or curling the ball into the net from impossible angles, Henry was a player in a league of his own.

But soccer isn't a one-person sport, and the beauty of this Arsenal team was how every player seemed to find their best form. In midfield, there was Patrick Vieira, a towering figure whose long strides covered the grass like it was his own personal domain. He could stop an opposing player in their tracks with a tackle as easily as he could launch an attack with a perfectly placed pass.

At the back, the defense was marshaled by Sol Campbell, a player whose name struck respect into any forward daring to challenge him. Beside him, the likes of Kolo Touré and Ashley Cole added speed and tenacity. Each of them played with a shared heartbeat, a rhythm that seemed to pulse through the team whenever they stepped onto the pitch.

And in goal stood Jens Lehmann, the German goalkeeper whose acrobatic saves were as much a part of

Arsenal's strength as the goals they scored. Lehmann's reflexes often turned what looked like a certain goal into a moment of awe, with the ball somehow, almost magically, kept out of the net.

As the season unfolded, Arsenal started to pick up speed like a train whose engineer had just spotted the green light of an open track. Match after match, they left stations behind - sometimes with the smoothness of a commuter express, sometimes with the gritty determination of a freight train battling uphill.

Victories were collected like precious gems, each one adding to a treasure that was becoming more and more apparent. The fans began to whisper about the possibility, the players began to dream it in their hearts, and the manager began to see it in their eyes.

But a quest like this is never without its tests. Arsenal faced down every challenge, from the snow of winter matches to the springtime bloom of rival teams hoping to halt their progress. They had close calls, nail-biting finishes, and moments where the dream seemed to hang by a thread.

The beautiful soccer that Wenger so believed in was a joy to behold. Passes were strung together like pearls on a necklace, with each movement bringing a new luster to their play. And through it all, they adhered to their philosophy: to play soccer with creativity, courage, and an unyielding desire to be the best.

As Arsenal's journey through the season continued, each match added a new chapter to their unfolding story. The team wasn't just winning; they were captivating the hearts of fans with a style of soccer that was both effective and enchanting. They played with a flair that was reminiscent of a well-conducted orchestra — every pass, every move, and every goal was a note in a symphony of sport.

One of the pivotal moments came in the deep chill of winter, under the floodlights that turned night into day on the pitch. Arsenal was up against Manchester United, a team with their own rich history and a fierce will to win. It was a clash of titans, a true test of Arsenal's mettle. The tension could be felt in the electric air that buzzed around the stadium, where every shout and cheer was magnified.

As the whistle blew, the game unfurled with an intensity that matched the occasion. Each tackle was sharp, each run was full of purpose, and the ball zipped across the field as though it was desperate to be part of this historic campaign. The Gunners showed their class, maintaining composure even as the Red Devils pressed hard, looking for a crack in Arsenal's armor.

It was in this game that Arsenal's defensive solidity was put to the ultimate test. Manchester United attacked in waves, but each time they thought they had a glimpse of goal, it was snuffed out by the relentless Arsenal backline or thwarted by the imposing presence of Lehmann in goal.

But the Gunners were not just about defense. When they won the ball, they transformed defense into attack with a fluidity that was breathtaking. Henry, with his ability to turn a defender inside out, scored a goal that would be replayed in highlight reels for years to come. It was a goal that captured the essence of Arsenal's season: audacious, skillful, and sublime.

As the final whistle blew, securing a victory for Arsenal, the sense of destiny grew stronger. This wasn't just another win; it was a statement. Arsenal weren't just part of the title race — they were leading it, and they were doing so with a grace that made their potential unbeaten season seem like a work of art in motion.

The weeks rolled by, and the wins kept coming. The beautiful game was on full display every time Arsenal played. Each match was not just a contest but a celebration of soccer at its finest. The camaraderie within the team was evident to all; they were a band of brothers, united in their quest for glory. Wenger often spoke about playing with belief and joy, and his team was the embodiment of that philosophy.

Players like Robert Pires and Freddie Ljungberg became heroes, not just for their goals but for their unselfish play and their unwavering commitment to the team's ethos. Their midfield wizardry and their knack for turning up at the right place at the right time added an extra layer of thrill to Arsenal's performances.

As the season drew towards its climax, the question on everyone's lips was not if Arsenal could win the title, but if they could complete the season unbeaten—a feat not seen for over a century in English soccer.

Each game now was not just about the three points at stake but about etching their names into the eternal story of the sport. With every game that passed without defeat, the dream edged closer to becoming a stunning reality. But in soccer, as in any sport, nothing is certain until the final whistle of the final game.

As the season marched on, the numbers started to tell a tale of their own. Arsenal's stats were not just impressive—they were becoming historic. By the time spring had unfolded its colors across England, Arsenal had notched up an incredible 26 games without defeat. Their tally of wins was astounding, and with each match, they extended their lead at the top of the Premier League table.

The stats showcased not just the quantity of victories but the quality of soccer Arsenal played. They had scored over 70 goals, a testament to their attacking prowess. Players like Thierry Henry and Dennis Bergkamp contributed heavily to this tally, with Henry netting 30 goals alone in the league. The team's passing accuracy was another point of pride, often exceeding 80% in matches, showcasing their control and dominance in play.

On the defensive side, the team was just as formidable. Jens Lehmann, the German goalkeeper, had kept more than 10 clean sheets, and the defensive quartet in front of him, led by Sol Campbell and Kolo Touré, were a wall that few could penetrate. The team conceded fewer than 30 goals throughout their campaign, an impressive feat that underlined their all-around strength.

As they approached the final stretch, the pressure was palpable. Could they maintain this staggering form? The media dissected their remaining fixtures, and fans scrutinized every potential hurdle that could upset their historic journey. Each match was now a mixture of nervous anticipation and exhilarating soccer.

One particular game stood out, a match against fierce rivals Tottenham Hotspur. It wasn't just a North London derby with the usual bragging rights at stake; it was a match that could solidify Arsenal's invincible status. The atmosphere was a blend of excitement and anxiety, with fans aware they were potentially watching history in the making.

The game itself was a microcosm of their season. Arsenal went behind early but showed their characteristic resilience to fight back. Goals from Patrick Vieira and Robert Pires turned the game on its head. The match ended 2-2, a draw that was enough to see Arsenal crowned as Premier League champions with four games to spare. But the champagne was on ice — the unbeaten record was still in play.

With each of the remaining games, Arsenal edged closer to immortality. The press coverage was intense, the discussion among soccer pundits was incessant, and the public's imagination was captured. Kids in parks pretended to be Henry or Bergkamp, dreaming of their own undefeated seasons.

Finally, on a sunny May afternoon, in their last game of the season against Leicester City, Arsenal clinched the draw they needed. The final whistle blew, and the record was theirs: 38 games played, 26 wins, 12 draws, and a staggering 0 losses. They finished the season with 90 points, 11 points clear of second-placed Chelsea. They had not only won the Premier League but had done so without losing a single game, a feat last accomplished by Preston North End in 1889, and never before in the modern era.

The team had defied critics, exceeded expectations, and rewritten the soccer history books. 'The Invincibles', as they would come to be known, had secured their legacy—a legacy that would be talked about for generations to come.

As the jubilant fans celebrated and the players basked in the glory of their unmatched achievement, the significance of what they had accomplished began to set in. Arsenal's 'Invincibles' had not just won a title; they had set a standard that became the golden benchmark in soccer history. Their unbeaten run was more than a record; it was a powerful message about teamwork, perseverance, and the art of soccer. It inspired young players and fans around the world, becoming a story that transcended the sport itself. Years from now, children and adults alike would look back at the 2003-2004 Arsenal squad not just as champions, but as legends who captured the true spirit of the beautiful game, leaving an indelible mark on the hearts of millions.

CHAPTER 12:

Samba in Cleats: The Artistry of Neymar on the Pitch

In the vibrant nation of Brazil, where soccer pulses through the veins of its cities and samba beats set the rhythm of life, a young boy with a dazzling smile and a natural flair for the beautiful game began to make waves. His name? Neymar da Silva Santos Júnior, or simply Neymar to the world. He wasn't just another soccer player; he was a prodigy, a performer, a phenomenon on the pitch who could dance past defenders as if they were statues.

The story begins in the sun-drenched streets of São Vicente, São Paulo, where a young Neymar would kick a tattered ball with bare feet, dreaming of one day wearing the golden jersey of the Brazilian national team. The son of a former soccer player, Neymar inherited not just the passion for the sport but also a talent that seemed to be from another world.

Even as a child, Neymar's abilities were undeniable. He joined the youth ranks of Santos FC, a club renowned for nurturing the talent of Pelé, arguably the greatest soccer player of all time. By the age of 17, Neymar made his professional debut, and what a debut it was! He didn't just play; he mesmerized, showing a prowess that belied his young age. His skills were exceptional, his dribbles were hypnotic, and his goals? They were simply out of this world.

Neymar's first season with the senior team of Santos FC saw him find the net 14 times in 48 appearances, a remarkable start for the young player who was just introducing himself to the world of professional soccer. It wasn't just the quantity of the goals that caught everyone's attention, it was their quality – the audacious flicks, the cheeky chips, the solo runs that left defenders trailing in his wake. His second season was even more prolific, with Neymar scoring an impressive 42 goals in just 60 matches across all competitions, signaling the rise of Brazil's next great soccer star.

As his skillset expanded, so did his reputation. In 2010, at just 18, Neymar helped lead Santos to its first Copa do Brasil title in the club's history, scoring 11 goals throughout the tournament, including a critical goal in the final that secured the championship. This accomplishment was a testament to his rapidly burgeoning talent and his crucial role in the team's success.

In the following year, his contributions would become even more significant. Neymar played a pivotal role in

Santos's victory in the 2011 Copa Libertadores, South America's most prestigious club competition, which the club had not won since 1963 when the legendary Pelé was its star. Neymar was instrumental throughout the tournament, but particularly so in the final, where his goal in the first leg helped seal a victory for Santos. By the end of that season, Neymar had racked up a personal tally of 24 goals in 53 appearances, his name echoing around the world as one of the most exciting talents in soccer.

But Neymar was not just a goal-scoring machine; he was also a creative force. His ability to set up his teammates was evident in his impressive assist records, contributing to many more goals than he scored himself. With his flair and vision, Neymar was more than just a forward; he was a playmaker who could change the course of a game with a single touch.

These early years at Santos laid the groundwork for Neymar's legacy as not just a goal scorer, but as a player who brought artistry and joy to the pitch. He was not only a marvel to watch but also a statistical powerhouse who was racking up records and accolades, all before his 20th birthday.

Neymar's skills on the pitch quickly turned into the sort of stories that kids would kick around in the streets, trying to imitate his moves. They'd watch his games, jaws dropped, as he performed a rainbow flick over an opponent or darted past defenders with a ball seemingly glued to his feet. He wasn't just playing soccer; he was redefining the art of the sport with every match.

In 2012, Neymar received the South American Footballer of the Year award for the second time in a row, cementing his status as one of the brightest stars in soccer. His style was exhilarating, a mix of raw speed, impeccable control, and a boldness that turned each game into a highlight reel. With 43 goals in 47 games for Santos that year, his stats were not merely impressive; they were record-breaking. But Neymar's influence stretched far beyond numbers; he was becoming a symbol of the beautiful game played at its most audacious and entertaining.

The chatter about Neymar wasn't limited to Brazil. Europe's biggest clubs had been watching, and it wasn't long before he was linked with moves to the continent's most prestigious teams. Yet, Neymar's loyalty to Santos was unwavering, at least for a little while longer. He wanted to achieve something memorable with the club that had nurtured his talent, to give back to the fans who chanted his name from the stands.

In his final season with Santos, Neymar once again demonstrated why he was so sought after. His performances in the São Paulo State Championship were nothing short of breathtaking. He helped his team to victory, scoring in the final and being named the tournament's best player. His goal tally was formidable, but his creative output was also through the roof, providing numerous assists and playing a part in almost every goal Santos scored.

What set Neymar apart was his deep understanding of the game's rhythm. He could sense when to accelerate and when to slow things down, creating spaces that previously didn't exist and threading passes through the eye of a needle. Each game was like a masterclass in soccer tactics and execution, delivered by a player who seemed to operate on a different frequency than everyone else on the pitch.

As Neymar's time at Santos drew to a close, the anticipation of his next step was palpable. He had conquered Brazil, and now it was time to take on a new challenge. His legacy at Santos was etched firmly into the fabric of the club, a tale of a hometown hero who danced his way through defenses and into the hearts of soccer fans around the world. The boy with the golden touch from São Paulo was ready to spread his wings, and the world of soccer eagerly awaited the next chapter of Neymar's journey.

The year 2013 marked a turning point in Neymar's career. After much speculation and anticipation, he announced his move to Barcelona, a club synonymous with mesmerizing football and home to some of the greatest players in history. The transfer was one of the most talked-about in soccer, and expectations were sky-high for the young Brazilian wonder.

Arriving in Spain, Neymar was stepping into a new realm. Barcelona's playing style, with its tiki-taka passes and emphasis on possession, was different from the free-flowing, attacking samba style he had grown up with. But Neymar's adaptability was as impressive as his dribbling. He quickly gelled with his new teammates, among them the legendary Lionel Messi and the crafty Andrés Iniesta. His debut season was a flurry of learning and integration, and while Barcelona did not clinch the La Liga title, Neymar's contributions were noteworthy. He scored 9 goals and provided 8 assists in the league, a promising start for the newcomer.

The 2014/2015 season was a showcase of Neymar's blossoming talent. Under the guidance of coach Luis Enrique, Neymar, Messi, and Luis Suárez — a trio that would come to be known as 'MSN' — formed an attacking force that was the envy of clubs worldwide. Neymar's speed and agility, combined with his natural flair, complemented his teammates' skills perfectly. Together, they scored a staggering 122 goals across all competitions, propelling Barcelona to a historic treble — winning La Liga, the Copa del Rey, and the UEFA Champions League.

Neymar's statistics for the season were extraordinary. He scored 22 goals in La Liga and 10 in the Champions

League, including a crucial goal in the final against Juventus, sealing a 3-1 victory for Barcelona. His performances earned him third place in the FIFA Ballon d'Or ranking, behind only his teammate Messi and Cristiano Ronaldo. It was clear that Neymar had not just joined the ranks of the elite; he was now a pivotal player on one of the best teams in the world.

In the seasons that followed, Neymar's star continued to rise. His ability to take on defenders one-on-one, to find the back of the net from seemingly impossible angles, and to pull off no-look passes and cheeky nutmegs kept fans on the edge of their seats. By the end of his tenure at Barcelona, Neymar had played 186 games, scoring 105 goals and delivering numerous assists. His synergy with Messi and Suárez had reached telepathic levels, with the trio leading Barcelona to further glory, including consecutive domestic doubles.

Yet, even amidst all the success, the desire for a new challenge grew within Neymar. He was ready to step out from the shadows of the Camp Nou giants and carve his own path to greatness. This desire culminated in his record-breaking transfer to Paris Saint-Germain in 2017, a move that shocked the soccer world and started a new chapter in Neymar's illustrious career. His legacy at Barcelona, however, was secured, marked by an exhilarating blend of Brazilian artistry and Catalan precision that would be remembered for generations to come.

As the curtains closed on Neymar's chapter at Barcelona, the impact he had made was enormous. His time at the club was more than a collection of individual highlights; it was a period of growth, of challenge, and of triumphs that left a mark on the hearts of fans and on the history of the club.

His move to Paris Saint-Germain was met with a mixture of awe and disbelief, as the world's most expensive transfer. This was Neymar's statement of intent, his quest to emerge not just as a global icon, but as a leader, ready to take the central role on a new stage.

Looking back at his time in Spain, it's the blend of Neymar's audacious talent and the maturity he gained that stands out. In the storied blue and red jersey of Barcelona, he danced past defenders with the joy and abandon of a child at play, yet his game carried the weight of a seasoned maestro when it mattered most.

Neymar's story at Barcelona is a testament to the beautiful game's power to kindle the imagination of people everywhere, especially the young fans who see in his journey the footprints of dreams made tangible. It's a tale of a young boy from Santos who reached the stars, not by dimming his brilliance, but by sharing it with the world, lighting up stadiums across continents with his exuberant play and boundless passion.

CHAPTER 13:

A FIFA Fairytale: Japan and the 2011 Women's World Cup

The year was 2011, and the Women's World Cup was about to witness one of the most remarkable underdog stories in its history. The protagonists of our tale? The Nadeshiko Japan, the national women's soccer team of Japan.

The odds were not in Japan's favor. They were considered a competent, disciplined team, but not one likely to make it to the top. Their group was tough, but they emerged successful, winning two games and losing only one. Every match was a battle, and they were ready to fight.

It wasn't just about skill or strategy; it was about heart. In the quarterfinals, they faced the host nation, Germany, a team many had picked to win the tournament. The match was intense, with Germany dominating possession and Japan holding their ground, countering when they could. The minutes ticked by without a goal, and the match went into extra time. Then, in the 108th minute, the unexpected happened. Karina Maruyama received a through ball and, with incredible composure, slotted it past the German goalkeeper. Japan had done the impossible and knocked out the favorites!

The semifinals were against Sweden, another tough opponent. The Swedes took the lead early, but Japan did not lose spirit. Instead, they answered with three goals, each a display of teamwork and determination. The final score was 3-1 to Japan. They were headed to the final — a first in their history.

But the most remarkable part of their story wasn't just the victories. It was what these victories meant. Japan was still reeling from the devastating earthquake and tsunami that struck earlier that year, and the team had become a symbol of hope for their nation. They weren't just playing for themselves; they were playing for every single person back home who was trying to rebuild their lives.

The final awaited, and with it, a chance to make their fairytale complete.

The stage was set for a dramatic conclusion to Japan's journey. The final of the 2011 FIFA Women's World Cup saw them face a formidable opponent: the United States, a powerhouse with stars like Abby Wambach and Hope Solo. The U.S. team was chasing their own dream, eager to claim their first World Cup title since 1999. The match was not just a clash of teams but of contrasting soccer philosophies: the physical, direct play of the Americans versus the technical, patient approach of the Japanese.

As the game commenced, fans around the world were glued to their screens. Japan fell behind twice, and twice they mustered the strength to equalize. The determination of the Nadeshiko was palpable. Ayumi Kaihori, Japan's goalkeeper, made a series of stunning saves to keep their hopes alive. The U.S. team was relentless, but the Japanese defense, anchored by the indomitable Saki Kumagai, held firm.

In the 81st minute, with Japan trailing 1-0, Aya Miyama was in the right place at the right time, pouncing on a mistake by the U.S. defense to poke the ball into the net. The match went to extra time, where once again the U.S. took the lead, a powerful header by Wambach making it 2-1. But with just three minutes left in extra time, Homare Sawa, Japan's inspirational captain, flicked in a corner with her heel, sending the game to penalties.

The statistics didn't favor Japan; the U.S. had never lost a World Cup game in which Wambach scored. But stats can only tell you so much. Soccer, like any sport, is unpredictable—it's why we watch, why we cheer, why we believe.

The penalty shootout was a nail-biter. Kaihori made a stunning save, and another U.S. shot hit the crossbar. The weight of the moment was immense, and when Saki

Kumagai stepped up for Japan's final penalty, she bore it with the same composure they had shown throughout the tournament. She scored, sealing a 3-1 shootout victory and crowning Japan as World Champions for the first time in history.

Their victory was a testament to their technical skills, yes, but also to their mental strength. They had faced adversity with a smile, played every game with joy, and never gave up, no matter the score. They showed that in soccer, as in life, the heart can carry you through when the odds are stacked against you.

The stats were remarkable — Japan had won the World Cup having never led at any point in the knockout stage until the final whistle of the penalty shootout. Sawa ended the tournament with five goals, earning her both the Golden Boot as the top scorer and the Golden Ball as the tournament's best player. But beyond the numbers, it was the spirit of the team that captivated the world. Japan's triumph was more than just a sports victory; it was a narrative of resilience and hope that transcended the soccer field.

The story of Japan's 2011 Women's World Cup victory is not just one of athletic prowess; it's a tale of a nation finding joy amidst hardship. Earlier that year, Japan had been devastated by a massive earthquake and tsunami, a disaster that shook the country to its core. The Nadeshiko became a symbol of hope and resilience for their nation, playing not only for the glory of victory but to lift the spirits of their compatriots.

Throughout the tournament, each player carried the weight of this purpose, understanding that every dribble, every pass, and every goal was for something greater than themselves. Their coach, Norio Sasaki, used images from the disaster to remind them of what they were playing for — unity, strength, and the indomitable human spirit.

As the celebrations began and confetti rained down on the champions, it was clear that this victory was felt deeply by everyone back home. In sports bars and living rooms across Japan, fans cried tears of joy, embracing each other. The win was more than a game; it was a moment of collective catharsis.

On their return, the players were greeted as heroes. The images of their triumph — Kaihori's diving saves, Sawa's sly flick, and Kumagai's decisive penalty — were etched into the nation's collective memory. Schools and clubs reported a surge in girls signing up to play soccer, wanting to emulate their new heroes. The impact of their victory rippled through the society, sowing seeds for the future of women's soccer in Japan.

In the years to follow, the legacy of the 2011 team continued to inspire. The Nadeshiko became a household name, their style of play analyzed and admired. The blend of technical skill, strategic intelligence, and unwavering spirit set a new standard for what a team could achieve.

Statistically, Japan's victory was against the odds — the United States was ranked number one in the world and had never lost to Japan in 25 previous encounters. But the Japanese team had shown that in soccer, the game isn't played on paper, and it certainly isn't won by statistics alone. It's played with heart, with belief, and with an unwavering commitment to each other and to the game.

As the years have passed, the story of the 2011 Women's World Cup remains a favorite tale. It is recounted not just for the remarkable soccer played or for the accolades and statistics accrued but for its embodiment of the power of sports to unite, to heal, and to bring joy. It's a reminder to all young soccer enthusiasts that sometimes, the underdog emerges victorious, not by chance, but through the strength of spirit and the unity of a team with a common dream.

CHAPTER 14:

Madeira to Madrid: The Making of Christiano Ronaldo

On the sunny island of Madeira, Portugal, where the Atlantic Ocean brushes against rugged cliffs and verdant hills, a young boy named Cristiano Ronaldo began his journey. Ronaldo wasn't born into the luxury of sports academies or high-tech training facilities. His first football wasn't store-bought; it was made from rags stitched together, but for young Cristiano, it might as well have been a treasure.

Growing up, Ronaldo's home life was simple, his family not wealthy. His father worked as a kit man at a local club, and it was here, on the uneven fields where his father toiled, that Ronaldo learned to play, his feet dancing over the grass with a football that seemed to be a part of him. He played for hours, every kick and dribble fueled by a dream that was as big as his talent.

Ronaldo's skill with the ball was apparent early on, and by the age of just 10, he was already catching the eyes of some of Portugal's biggest clubs. He didn't have the polished boots or the fancy gear, but what he did have was a relentless work ethic and a natural ability that couldn't be ignored.

By the age of 12, he made a life-changing move to Sporting Lisbon's academy, hundreds of miles from his family. It was a brave step, one filled with challenges and the kind of homesickness that could bring a grown man to tears. But Ronaldo's determination never wavered; he trained hard, pushing his body and honing his skills, dreaming of one day taking to the field in one of Europe's grand stadiums.

His performances for Sporting Lisbon's youth teams were nothing short of remarkable. He scored at a pace that made people take notice, and his dribbles and tricks were like those of players much older. Ronaldo's name started to echo in the conversations of soccer fans and scouts across Europe.

The stats started to build even then, with Ronaldo scoring two goals on his league debut for the first team at only 17 years old. His rise was rapid, and it wasn't long before the biggest clubs in the world came calling.

At 18 years old, Ronaldo faced a moment that would change his life forever. In a friendly match against one of England's most storied clubs, Manchester United, Ronaldo played with such skill, such speed, and such artistry that even the opposing team's players urged their manager to sign him. And so, in 2003, Cristiano Ronaldo, the boy from Madeira who once played with a rag football, found himself in the red jersey of Manchester United, ready to conquer the soccer world.

The English Premier League was tough, known for its physical play and fast pace, but Ronaldo adapted. He didn't just adapt, actually—he thrived. His first season brought challenges, and some critics doubted him, but he responded in the way he knew best: by working harder and playing better. He transformed his body, building strength to match his skill, and by his second season, he was a force to be reckoned with.

His stats began to sparkle. He scored goals that took the breath away, delivered assists that were talked about for weeks, and showed a flair on the pitch that turned him into a fan favorite. By the age of 23, Ronaldo had helped Manchester United to three Premier League titles in a row and had won his first Ballon d'Or—an award given to the world's best player.

But stats only tell part of the story. Ronaldo's influence went beyond goals and assists; he was changing the game. His speed and technique pushed defenders to their limits, forcing them to adapt. Off the field, his dedication to training and fitness set new standards. Young players all over the world looked up to him, not just for his soccer prowess but for his discipline and work ethic.

During his time at Manchester United, Ronaldo's numbers were impressive. He scored over 100 goals for the club, a remarkable feat for a winger, not a traditional striker whose main role is to score. In the 2007-2008 season, he found the net 42 times in all competitions, a statistic that helped earn him that year's Ballon d'Or.

Ronaldo's journey was like a storybook tale, but it wasn't just about talent. It was about dedication, perseverance, and the courage to chase a dream, no matter how far from home it took him. With every goal, every victory, he showed what was possible with belief and hard work.

Ronaldo's six-year spell at Manchester United was coming to an end, but it wasn't just a chapter closing in a book; it was the beginning of a new saga. In 2009, he made a move that was talked about in playgrounds, cafés, and living rooms all over the world. Ronaldo signed for Real Madrid, the Spanish club known for its galaxy of stars, for a record-breaking transfer fee. It was a move that set expectations sky-high, and Ronaldo was ready to leap even higher.

At Real Madrid, Ronaldo's star burned even brighter. He stepped onto the pitch at the Santiago Bernabéu Stadium, ready to show that every euro spent on him was worth it. And did he ever show it! His goal-scoring feats reached new heights. He wasn't just scoring goals; he was breaking records. In Spain, they call it 'hacer historia' or 'making history', and that's what Ronaldo was doing. He became the fastest player to reach 100 goals in the Spanish league, a record that had fans rubbing their eyes in disbelief.

But here's the thing about Ronaldo: he wasn't a solo act. He believed in teamwork and leadership. He wore the captain's armband with pride, and when he lifted trophies, he always spoke about the effort of the team. He led Real Madrid to two La Liga titles and, perhaps most impressively, four UEFA Champions League trophies, including three in a row, a feat that seemed almost superhuman.

In his nine seasons with Real Madrid, Ronaldo's stats were otherworldly. He scored an astonishing 450 goals in 438 appearances, a rate that seems almost like a misprint. But it's true. He scored more goals than he played games! He also provided numerous assists, showing that he could create opportunities for his teammates just as much as he could finish them himself.

Off the pitch, Ronaldo's impact was just as strong. He became a global icon, a symbol of excellence in sport. His face was on billboards, his name on the back of countless jerseys worn by aspiring young soccer players, and his social media accounts followed by millions.

But even icons have to face challenges, and Ronaldo was no different. He dealt with injuries, with intense media scrutiny, and the pressure of always being expected to be the best. Through it all, he remained focused, showing that it's not just talent that gets you to the top—it's the ability to keep going, even when the going gets tough.

As Ronaldo's chapter at Real Madrid came to a close, his legacy was etched not only in the record books but also in the hearts of fans around the globe. He left behind a trail of unforgettable moments, from breathtaking goals to displays of camaraderie and sportsmanship that transcended the competitive nature of the sport. His dedication to his craft, his team, and his fans was evident in every match he played.

In 2018, Ronaldo decided it was time for a new adventure, this time in Italy with Juventus. His departure from Real Madrid was the end of an era, but also a testament to his relentless pursuit of growth and new challenges. At Juventus, he continued to demonstrate why he's considered one of the greatest, not just by maintaining his incredible performance but also by adapting to a new league and style of play, proving that his skills were universal.

Ronaldo's journey from a young talent in Madeira to a global soccer icon is a story of determination, resilience, and an unwavering belief in oneself. It serves as an inspiration to children and adults alike that with hard work and passion, any dream is attainable. The tale of

Cristiano Ronaldo is not just about soccer; it's a narrative that teaches the value of setting goals, staying disciplined, and always striving to be the best version of oneself.

For kids around the world, Ronaldo's story is a beacon of hope and a reminder that talent can take you far, but it's the heart and hard work that take you further. He's not just a player; he's a role model who shows what it means to never give up on your dreams, no matter how big they seem.

CHAPTER 15:

Goalkeeping Glory: Tim Howard's Record-Breaking World Cup Performance

In the sprawling suburbs of North Brunswick, New Jersey, a young boy with boundless energy and an unstoppable spirit was busy laying the foundations for a record-breaking future. Tim Howard, born on March 6, 1979, wasn't just any kid; he was a whirlwind of determination with a soccer ball at his feet, and a pair of gloves that seemed to magnetically attract the ball.

From a tender age, Tim faced more challenges than most of his peers. He was diagnosed with Tourette syndrome, a condition that manifests through involuntary movements and vocal sounds. But even as a child, Tim never saw this as a hindrance. Instead, it became part of his unique rhythm, a cadence that he brought to the soccer field. His energy was endless, and his focus, once channeled, was impenetrable. This combination made him a force to be reckoned with, especially when he stood between the goalposts, his eyes tracking every movement of the ball like a hawk.

Tim's love for soccer was kindled in the streets and fields of his hometown, where he played with a joyous abandon and a competitive edge that drew the attention of coaches and players alike. It wasn't long before his raw talent and sheer dedication landed him a spot on the Central Jersey Cosmos, a local youth team that would be the first to polish the rough diamond that was his goalkeeping prowess.

In those early days, Tim's reflexes were as sharp as they were intuitive. He seemed to have a sixth sense for where the ball would go, a talent that would serve him well throughout his career. Every save was a battle won, and with each game, the young keeper's reputation grew. His hands, already strong and sure, became the last line of defense for his team, swatting away shots that seemed destined for the back of the net.

His journey from the local soccer fields to the world stage was not a straight path—it was one filled with hurdles, hard work, and the kind of heart that doesn't understand the meaning of 'give up'. Tim Howard's tale isn't just about the saves he made, but the mindset with which he made them. It's a story about not just stopping goals, but about how a young man from New Jersey became a symbol of hope and a testament to the idea that greatness can be achieved no matter the odds.

As Tim Howard grew older, his presence on the soccer field became more pronounced, his skills more refined.

The numbers began to tell a story of success; every game he played added to his burgeoning reputation. By the time he was a teenager, Tim was already standing out, his clean sheets — games where he prevented the opposition from scoring — not just a testament to his skill but a beacon of his potential.

When he was just 19 years old, he made a move that would be the first significant step in his professional career, joining the MetroStars, a Major League Soccer (MLS) team known today as the New York Red Bulls. The stats from his early days were promising; over the six seasons with the MetroStars, Tim accumulated a total of 13 shutouts. These numbers, though not earth-shattering, were indicative of a keeper who was just warming up.

But it wasn't until his leap across the pond to the storied grounds of Manchester United in 2003 that his talent truly began to crystallize into something exceptional. At one of the most high-profile clubs in the world, Tim's goalkeeping abilities would be put to the test. He rose to the challenge, securing 10 clean sheets in his 32 Premier League appearances in his debut season. This impressive start in English football spoke volumes about Tim's capabilities and the impact he was destined to have on the game.

While Tim's career had its ups and downs — facing competition for his spot at Manchester United and eventually moving to Everton — his stats continued to build a compelling narrative. At Everton, he found his home, becoming a fan favorite and a consistent performer. Over the 10 seasons with the Toffees, Tim notched up an incredible 132 clean sheets in all competitions. His reliability and shot-stopping prowess made him a cornerstone of the team's defense, contributing significantly to Everton's successes during his tenure.

Yet, it would be during the 2014 FIFA World Cup where Tim Howard would etch his name into the history books. On July 1, 2014, in a round of 16 matches against Belgium, he delivered a performance for the ages. Tim made a record-breaking 15 saves, the most by any goalkeeper in a World Cup match since the recording of stats began in 1966. The sheer volume of saves was a testament to his reflexes, agility, and the indomitable spirit that had been his trademark since his youth. Despite the United States losing the match 2-1 after extra time, Tim's heroics won him worldwide acclaim and highlighted his incredible contribution to the sport.

Tim Howard's career, marked by the countless shots he has stopped and the many games where he has kept the opposition at bay, tells a story of dedication, resilience, and unmatched goalkeeping talent. His journey from the playgrounds of New Jersey to the world's greatest soccer stages embodies the spirit of perseverance and is a powerful reminder to young fans everywhere that no matter the obstacles, with hard work and belief, anything is possible.

As the echoes of applause for his record-breaking World Cup performance faded, Tim Howard continued to build on his legacy. The numbers he posted were more than just marks on a stat sheet; they told the story of a player whose determination and skill had propelled him to the apex of his sport. Every dive to make a save, every leap to punch the ball clear was a chapter in his epic tale.

In the following years, Tim would return to play for the Colorado Rapids in MLS, the league where he had first made his mark. His presence between the posts was as reassuring as ever to teammates and fans alike. He maintained his high standards, becoming a bulwark for the club and bringing his wealth of experience from European football back to American soil. Through the remainder of his playing days, Howard continued to awe fans with his shot-stopping ability and leadership on the field.

As he hung up his gloves, Tim Howard's impact on soccer was indelible. His journey from the lively fields of North Brunswick to the grand stadiums of international soccer was a beacon of hope and inspiration. It was a journey punctuated by jaw-dropping saves, awe-inspiring performances, and a World Cup outing that would be spoken of for generations to come.

The story of Tim Howard is a testament to the power of dreams and the unyielding human spirit. It's a reminder to every young soccer enthusiast clutching a ball and imagining their name emblazoned on a jersey that with heart, passion, and perseverance, they too can leave an indelible mark on the beautiful game.

Tim Howard's record-breaking day, his unshakable presence on the field, and his journey as a goalkeeper extraordinaire had not just made him a legend; they had made him a hero to many. His stats and figures in the game of soccer were impressive, but it was the immeasurable impact on the hearts of fans and aspiring goalkeepers worldwide that truly defined his legacy. The boy from New Jersey had become 'The Secretary of Defense', a title befitting the courage and heroism he displayed on and off the pitch.

Made in United States
Troutdale, OR
06/04/2024

20297920R00060